AFTERMATH
A FIREFIGHTER'S LIFE

AFTERMATH

BRYAN RATUSHNIAK A FIREFIGHTER'S LIFE

Cormorant Books

The publisher gratefully acknowledges the support of the
Canada Council for the Arts and the Ontario Arts Council for its
publishing program. We acknowledge the financial support of the
Government of Canada through the Canada Book Fund (CBF) for our
publishing activities, and the Government of Ontario through Ontario Creates,
an agency of the Ontario Ministry of Culture,
and the Ontario Book Publishing Tax Credit Program.

LIBRARY AND ARCHIVES CANADA CATALOGUING IN PUBLICATION

Title: Aftermath : a firefighter's life / Bryan Ratushniak.
Names: Ratushniak, Bryan, author.
Identifiers: Canadiana (print) 20190234857 | Canadiana (ebook) 20190234865 |
ISBN 9781770865761 (softcover) | ISBN 9781770865778 (HTML)
Subjects: LCSH: Ratushniak, Bryan. |
LCSH: Fire fighters—Ontario—Toronto—Biography. |
LCSH: Fire fighters—Job stress. | LCSH: Fire fighters—Psychology. |
LCGFT: Autobiographies.
Classification: LCCTH9118.R38 A3 2020 | DDC 363.37092—dc23

Cover photo and design: Angel Guerra / Archetype
Interior text design & illustration: Tannice Goddard, tannicegdesigns.ca
Printer: Friesens

Printed and bound in Canada.

CORMORANT BOOKS INC.
260 SPADINA AVENUE, SUITE 502, TORONTO, ON M5T 2E4
www.cormorantbooks.com

Dedicated to the men and women of the
emergency services who may be struggling.

AFTERMATH
A FIREFIGHTER'S LIFE

1

The End of a Career

I MADE IT TO RETIREMENT after thirty-two years and one month on the job (the extra month was so I could squeeze in a final birthday before I threw in the towel). The last year or so had been tough mentally. Physically I had the usual aches and pains a firefighter suffers: bad back, sore knees, and pain in my elbows from torn muscles and ligament damage. And sleeping was getting difficult as traumatic memories increasingly snuck into my head at bedtime.

I felt as if I had overdosed on dead people. I was really tired of seeing death over and over again. It wasn't just the gross, messy deaths that result from traffic accidents or subway suicides that bothered me, but also the everyday kind of dying that a firefighter sees on the job: the ninety-year-old gentleman who died in his sleep, the seventy-five-year-old woman who died of cancer. I was taking on the grief and sadness that surrounded every passing of a loved one. I was struggling mentally. I couldn't face the death anymore — I'd had my fill.

I began taking time off work. I wasn't sure how much more mental anguish I could stand. I really loved fighting fires, but even that was becoming more difficult. I had recently started taking blood pressure medication for a previously undetected arrhythmia, found by accident during a routine cardiac stress test. As a result, the extreme physical exertion from firefighting became debilitating.

One night before a scheduled shift, I told my wife Sue that I felt trepidation about going in to work. Anxiety. She told me to see how I felt in the morning, and if I was still anxious I could book the day off if I needed to. The next morning the alarm went off at five, as it always did before a shift. I lay in bed, deciding whether I was strong enough to face work. I wasn't, but I also wasn't about to get Sue worrying about me fearing my job.

On my way to the fire hall I was blasting seventies rock on the car radio. I was stuck in the past I guess, reliving rock's heyday. Maybe I was reliving my teenage dreams of being a rock star. On the road up ahead, obscured by the glare of headlights, I could see what looked like something lying on the tracks in front of a street-car. Maybe it was a large carpet or building material that fell off the back of a truck.

As I changed lanes to bypass the obstruction, I could see the silhouettes of two people standing over whatever was in the road. As I got closer, I saw that it was a motorcycle lying on its side, next to a motionless person on the ground. I pulled the car over, put on the emergency flashers, and ran over to see if I could help.

A man was standing over the motorcyclist, talking to a 911 operator on his phone.

He told me the bike had smashed head-on into the front of the streetcar. The motorcyclist lay on his back, motionless, with an obvious head injury. I checked his pulse — he was VSA (vital signs absent). I started chest compressions and advised the man with the phone to update the 911 dispatcher that CPR was in progress, administered by a fire department captain on his way to work.

The crew from the fire hall just around the corner responded and arrived within a couple of minutes. I updated the firefighters about the patient's condition as they took over the life-saving efforts. I then cleaned myself up at the fire truck, thanked the crew, and continued on to the fire hall for my shift. I was shaken. I was trying to convince myself that I wasn't, but I was shaken.

A couple of hours into my shift, I received a call from the fire department information officer. A close friend of the motorcycle victim had called him and wanted to know if she could talk to me. I assured the information officer that I would be fine with that. In my mind, though, I just wanted to get rid of the thought of another life taken too early, someone else I had failed to save. I wanted to forget the whole traumatic affair, but I called her anyway.

The woman had known the victim very well — he was her fiancé's best friend. He had been scheduled to speak at their upcoming wedding. Her fiancé was taking the death of his friend very hard. He wanted to meet me, to thank me for trying to help and for being with his best friend when he died.

I met them both and passed on my condolences. I went to the man's funeral. I met his mother. She thanked me too. She took a photo of me to send to her family overseas who couldn't make it to the service. As someone who never again wanted to see death, I took it on the chin. They were grieving, they were hurting.

And I was too. At that same time, my sister was dying of cancer. I knew the pain the man's family and friends were feeling. I hoped that, when the time came for my sister to be taken from us, I would also have someone who understood share in the grieving process.

I lost my sister Brenda six months later. It was the weekend of my fifty-third birthday. I began to ponder about the right time to pull the plug on my firefighting career.

On Brenda's birthday, six months after she passed, I was spending time at the cottage, remembering my funny sister. I was so proud of her when, at the age of fifty-three, she competed in her first fitness competition. When she was getting sicker, I asked her how she felt about the inevitable. "I feel so sad, so very sad," she said. "There are so many things I still want to do."

Brenda had been set to retire and was making plans for the future after thirty years as a social worker, years of devoting herself to helping people. When she retired she wanted to continue to help people, spiritually and physically, through yoga and massage. She had built her dream house with her loving partner, Dale. It was outfitted with a gym, a hot tub, and massage rooms for her next chapter in life: being the proprietor of her own spa.

Brenda didn't make it to the opening of her spa. She didn't make it to her daughter's wedding. Sitting by the lake watching the sunset, I decided then and there that on my next birthday I would pack it in. There was too much living that I still wanted to experience.

2

The Chip on My Shoulder

I'VE BEEN ACCUSED OF HAVING a chip on my shoulder, and I do. I guess it comes from low self-esteem or something. My main beef is when people get on the job and think it's going to be a cakewalk. So many men and women out there would give their eye teeth to become a firefighter, but they can't make the cut for one reason or another.

I had always wanted to be a firefighter, but after 9/11 a lot of young guys wanted the job just because they thought it would get them laid. They didn't actually care for the work part of the job. Those are the kind of guys who give working firefighters a bad name. You know the type — they wear the blue T-shirt with a fire logo splashed across it and introduce themselves as a firefighter before they mention their name.

Historically the job of putting out fires came out of necessity. Honourable men and women stepped up to help their communities, not because it was a fashionable occupation but because they saw themselves as protectors of their families and neighbours. At the turn of the previous century, firefighters basically lived at the firehouse and were allowed only one day off a week. The pay was poor and the job was tough. The men who came before me were rough and rugged, vulgar and single-minded. When the bell rang, you knew those firefighters were going to give it their all. They didn't quit until the job was done or until they dropped from exhaustion. They would get injured and they would get killed.

Even as a child I knew firefighting was dangerous, having seen a few men hurt at fires around town when I was growing up, but I was drawn to the adrenaline rush I could feel radiating off of the firefighters as they fought to save a building or home. Over the course of my career I had my share of injuries and experienced that amazing hit of endorphins and wonderful feeling of gratification that accompanies a job well done and I've felt the respect and admiration of many of the public. It's the best job in the world.

Back before I came on the job, firefighters rode on the back step of the fire truck, holding on for dear life, much like sanitation workers do today. Ironically, when I was a teenager I worked one summer as a garbage man/boy, holding on to the back for dear life while secretly pretending to be a firefighter riding a fire truck.

Ask any eight-year-old boy, and probably many eight-year-old girls, what they want to be when they grow up and the answer is quite likely to be "a fireman" or "a firefighter." Polls consistently show that firefighters, like nurses, are admired and trusted more than doctors, pharmacists, police, lawyers, or politicians.

So, for the most part, people admire and respect firefighters. My beef is with the snide attitude some people have towards firefighters. It comes mostly from men who either are jealous or have a girlfriend that's attracted to firefighters or maybe just think firefighters are blue-collar slugs who are beneath them.

At a dinner party I was once asked by one of these guys, "What did you do today? Play cards and watch TV?" My response to that sort of question usually varied, depending on how cynical they were and how much alcohol was flowing in my system.

"No, I scraped a woman's brains out of the treads of my boots. I listened to the screams of someone who had just lost their son or daughter, mother or father, brother or sister. I saw a little kid trying to do CPR on his dead mother." Or whatever else had happened that day.

When guys like that are nicely tucked into bed at home, firefighters are soaked to the skin with sweat. We freeze in the winter and suffer from heat exhaustion in the summer. How can you explain the feeling of getting lost in the smoke? That you might not be able to make it out before you run out of air? *Where do I go? How can I get out?* Why would anyone willingly do that over and over again? You might keep moisturizing cream for dry skin in your desk at work; in my locker I had a tub of Noxzema for steam burns to my neck.

How do you account for people throwing beer bottles and garbage off their balconies at the firefighters responding to their building? They're angry at the "establishment" but we are only there to help them.

How do you explain to a person who sits in an air-conditioned office that when firefighters book a day off sick, it's not because they have the sniffles but rather that they've twisted an ankle, strained a shoulder, or wrenched their back, and they don't want to jeopardize the lives of their brothers and sisters? You don't want your friends to get injured because you dropped the ladder or couldn't get up the stairs fast enough to help them. You don't want to find out too late that you're not able to get through the smoke to carry them out because you had too much false pride to admit your back is still hurt from the last time you injured it, and it's not quite healed enough for you to rely on. If you sit at a desk all day typing or talking on the phone, you can go to work with a limp and function just fine.

Yes, I have a chip on my shoulder, but it comes from frustration. Life has become a bombardment of information. Our lives have become so busy it can be a struggle just to keep going. Still, I wonder, if people really knew what emergency workers go through on a daily basis, would they begin to understand our frustrations and our occasional lack of empathy?

The life of a firefighter doesn't stop when he hangs up his helmet at the end of a day. It stays inside you, the hidden horror of the job that you can't reveal to your children. One day a little boy visiting the fire hall asked what the Vicks VapoRub in my pocket was for. I told him it was for when I got the sniffles in the winter, just like he would get from playing outside in the snow. I didn't tell him the real reason: emergency responders rub it under their noses to mask the smell of a decomposing body that stinks so much you feel like puking.

It pisses me off when I hear someone say firefighters get paid to sleep. It happens more than you'd think. They may doze, but they never close. It's a trade-off for all the cancers most firefighters die from. They get paid for their truncated life expectancy, along with the aches and pains and nightmares they have to live with. The job even screws up your marriage, because you can't tell your spouse why you are so pissed off at the world, and he or she will never understand how much you care about the guys on your truck.

3

The Firebug Gets His Wings

"THE SCHOOL BURNED DOWN!" SCREAMED my older sister Chereyl.

Her shrill voice hit my ear at the precise frequency needed to leave evidence of a bladder failure in my jammies. Not taking anything from an older sister to be the truth, I ran to the picture window in the living room. Mr. Shields and Uncle Ted from across the street had left home. Both were volunteer firefighters Hmmm. There might be some truth to that scream my sister had deafened me with.

Fires have had both a good and bad influence on me. The sickening things I've seen on the job, images I can't get out of my head, complicated the normal stresses of ordinary life. It screwed up my head, and it screwed up my married life. Having said that, I was fighting fires for more than thirty years and I still got a rush every time I crawled into a hot, stinky blaze.

The first time I actually got up close to feel the heat of a large fire was in the middle of a summer day in 1970 when Ball Motors went up in flames. I had dragged my three-year-old brother, Adrian, out to see it — along with half the town. (More people showed up than when we got our first Zamboni and it drove the length of Main Street, much like a visiting pope would have, complete with the arena guy, Charlie Kelner, waving to the throngs as only a local hero could.) The smoke obscured the sky with a black mushroom cloud. Tires and pressurized tanks inside the burning building exploded. The people watching the fire stood in shock. After all, I thought, this was Ball Motors, which sold the coolest cars with the fattest tires!

The scene appeared like chaos to my seven-year-old eyes. The firefighters seemed to be running in all directions, dragging hose, putting up ladders. Since this was a tiny mining town, the fire department was made up of volunteers, some of whom actually worked for the business currently engulfed in flames. That's where I heard the word *shit* used as a complete sentence for the first time in my life. I was engrossed.

While the fire continued to escalate, Mr. Cunningham — who lived across the road from Ball Motors — jumped in his truck with a look of horror on his face and sped down Main Street in the opposite direction of the fire causing townsfolk watching the blaze to jump out of his way and shake their collective heads at the old man's recklessness.

My kid brother cried a lot, I guess he was fearful of the huge, imposing plume of acrid smoke. Maybe it was the fact that the fire got so hot and we were standing so close that it threatened to melt our new polyester bell-bottoms. I just wanted him to stop crying. I didn't want to have to take him home and miss the unfolding of this catastrophe in front of me. Then, over the shouts of the firefighters, sounds of bending metal, and crashing timber the sputter of an ill-tuned motor began to build. The sound grew to a deafening roar and looking skyward, through the column of smoke, emerged Mr. Cunningham in his ancient float plane to water-bomb the building!

The barrage of water released from the plane's pontoons missed most of the flames and drenched some of the spectators, who seemed to welcome the cooling off, but absolutely *battered* the house across the street from the fire — Mr. Cunningham's house. It was madness! But at that moment, I was hooked! I wanted a piece of that kind of action. I wanted to be a firefighter!

My hometown was a dying mining town in Northwestern Ontario called Geraldton, two hundred miles from the nearest traffic light — and, more importantly for a growing boy-about-town, from a McDonald's. I admired all the firefighters when I was growing up. Our neighbours were firefighters: Uncle Ted Tarkka, who was the fire chief, and Mr. Shields. They lived next door to each other and it was they who managed to prevent the paint shop at Ball Motors (where they were both employed) from burning down. (They had answered the call to my burning school with much less success — more on that later.) They were everyday people the townsfolk relied upon to watch over their families. And the people you needed if you wanted a custom paint job for your new hot rod.

I lived directly across the street from them, at 911 First Street West. The significance of my home address didn't clue me in to my future calling as a firefighter. That's because the number to call to report a fire in Geraldton back in the 1960s was "o" to tell Elsie the operator to phone the firefighters. The firefighters — and they were all men back then — had special phones in their homes in addition to the ordinary black rotary-dial phones we mere mortals possessed. The special fire phone was still a black rotary phone, but it had a cool sticker on it with the emergency number.

In the days before cellphones or pagers, Geraldton's firefighters were dispatched by an air-raid siren bolted to the top of Town Hall. One wail alerted firefighters to a fire north of the tracks, two wails for in the town, and three wails were for a fire south of the bridge. It was up to the volunteer firefighters to spot the tell-tale signs of incomplete combustion (i.e. smoke) and race to the blaze before it took out a whole block. The whole system was complicated by the town's noon siren (for synchronizing your watch, I guess) and a ten o'clock curfew siren for us kids. God help you if you lived north of the tracks and your place was on fire at lunchtime.

It was in the winter of 1969 that I was fortunate enough to hear from Chereyl that Mr. Shields and Uncle Ted had unsuccessfully stopped my school from burning to the ground overnight. I was in grade two at the time and madly in love with my teacher, Miss Adams. She was a dead ringer for Marlo Thomas, from the hit 1960s TV show *That Girl*. She had long, beautiful black hair; a glowing smile; and she wore the hottest purple-and-orange mini-skirt outfit, complete with go-go boots and a hat that reminded me of a Jiffy Pop pan when all the kernels had popped. Every day in class was a flirt session, with me being the beneficiary of her coy smile and twinkling eyes. At least, as a kid in grade two, this is what I believed.

Apparently the fire had started in our classroom, and Miss Adams was overcome with guilt. I went to school the next day to see for myself. I couldn't tell how they figured it started in our classroom because where the school used to be was now just a black hole filled with metal chairs and desk legs.

"Hey, it's only a school. Not a big deal," I said to Miss Adams, the pile still smouldering. Without a word Miss Adams burst into tears and walked away. She appeared to be more concerned about the school burning down than I was.

As I passed the old Bickle Seagrave fire truck I wondered why she would ignore me, her favourite student, like that. I was just trying to help her get over the whole burned school thing. But she chose to be consoled in the arms of our ex-football-hero sixth-grade teacher, Mr. Lunberg. I was heartbroken. Love can be cruel.

Even though the demise of my school meant a happy future of watching TV and playing road hockey, I was kind of pissed off because I had lost my favourite Christmas present. (At first I didn't want this favourite present, because after I ripped off the wrapping paper, it was packed in a Playtex Cross Your Heart bra box.)

It was a pair of knitted slippers that tied up in front, sort of like a pair of Phentex elf boots, and I used them to slide down the hallway at home while playing indoor road hockey. What would I do now for indoor entertainment? Being pissed off about losing my coveted hall-hockey slippers was one thing, but the next week we ended up being shoved into the high school library, which put an end to my road hockey career.

Later that year I learned that burning buildings are not all fun and games. My realization of the destructive forces of fire occurred when my dad rushed in to wake up my mom early one winter morning and told her the Blue Bird Grill, where she worked, had burned down during the night. Times were tough. The mine had closed down, money was tight, and now Mom was out of work. No new skates for Bryan — at eight years old I was still jamming my feet into the same tiny, rusted skates I had worn when I was four. I maintain that the reason I have little claw feet today is because of that stupid fire.

MONEY REMAINED TIGHT FOR MANY years, and both Mom and Dad worked extra jobs to make ends meet. I had to try to be a cool eight-year-old hitting up the babes while sporting my sister Brenda's hand-me-downs. I could have refused to wear her jeans, but I had outgrown all mine and the legs were now several inches too short, making them classic "flood pants," so I relented and wore my sister's pants — except the stretchy capris with the zipper up the bum. Most of her clothes could pass for boys' stuff; this was the early 1970s and the hippy thing was still going strong, meaning that both sexes wore more or less the same clothes. But wearing Brenda's old clothing finally came to a head for me one winter.

I was outside with my friends during school recess playing "Jump on the Little Kid," which was basically football without a ball. A little kid would run through the playground and the bigger kids would chase him down and pile up on him. It was a very simple game that you could play all recess, basically chasing a little kid (usually me) and tackling him, working up a good sweat in the process. This time, coming up from the bottom of the pile, I had my winter parka unzipped to cool off, and the sweater I was wearing was stretched out of shape because some kid had grabbed it when he tackled me. Underneath, exposed for all to see, was the little bow at the top of my sister's undershirt.

John D saw the little pink bow and shouted this revelation at the top of his lungs. I denied this possibly world-ending information vehemently, but he had seen it.

I ran into the school washroom and tore the bow off my undershirt, praying to the gods above that John wouldn't blab and tell the rest of my friends who were out of ear shot of the initial discovery about it. That night, in a rage, I tore all the bows off my undershirts.

I can't blame John for tattling on me — eight-year-olds have the social skills of a chimpanzee. Sadly, John D died in a house fire a few years later. His body was found at the bottom of the stairs, burned so badly that when the firefighter tried to pick him up, the skin slid off his arm. (This is an experience I would become familiar with, and it feels as gross as it sounds.)

The shame and embarrassment I felt as all eyes on the playground zeroed in on my pink bow was the same torturous feeling I had experienced when I was in kindergarten. It was spring, and in art class our teacher, Mrs. Bridges, had given us drawings of pussy willows that we were to glue tufts of cotton batting onto. I was always eager to show Mom the art I had made in school that day, so with great zeal I placed generous tufts of cotton on each blob of glue. *Mom's going to love this*, I thought.

At the end of the class, just before we got ready to go home for the day, we handed our masterpieces in for Mrs. Bridges to set aside to dry. She looked at my pussy-willow picture and said coldly, "They're too big. Do it again," then started plucking off the tufts of cotton I had so expertly placed on the drawing.

The tears welled up in my eyes and my innate sense of rebellion instantly came to a boiling point. I shouted back at her, "Wendy Maclean has bigger pussy willows but you didn't wreck hers, because she's a girl!"

Mrs. Bridges handed back my sheet with little bits of cotton still stuck to the tiny bits of glue left after she'd mangled it. I redid it as quickly as I could, but the new, smaller pussy willows didn't stick very well. My project was ruined. Mom said it was nice anyway, even though I knew it looked brutal. Decades later I can still feel the humiliation of the moment.

4

An Explosive Year

IN THE SPRING OF 1974 I was eleven years old and had my eyes on the girls in earnest for the first time.

"Girls' lice! Girls' lice! You've got girls' lice!" a grubby-looking kid would shout as he punched me in the shoulder.

"No! My fingers were crossed!" I'd say, playing along but not really meaning the rebuttal. My fingers were never crossed, and I wanted to experience girls' lice for real.

The previous winter I had had my heart set on Penny Hunt. She was a foot taller than me, but I was quite the charmer and a handsome lad, too. *She will be mine*, I thought. *Oh yes, she will be mine.*

Because my family was struggling financially, Mom was frugal, a skill I didn't learn until a couple of divorces into my adult life. She would cut my hair rather than waste money on a barber. Normally you would expect your mom to butcher your hair and you'd have to wear a straw hat like my buddy Jay Samms did one summer, after his dad buzzed his long locks right to the skull, exposing a rash of mosquito bites on his noggin. But no, Mom cut my hair with expert precision so perfect it looked like a helmet.

During the winter, we kids would go skating at the arena on Friday nights. If you were serious about a girl, that was where you proclaimed it. The protocol of "date skating" was explained to me by David Gile: When you skated, you held the girl's hand. And if you were really serious, you touched shoulders as you skated. Wow, there were so many rules to this dating stuff.

I asked Penny to skate with me and she kindly permitted me to accompany her for a couple of turns. She even let me hold her hand, but when I tried to touch her shoulder with mine, I could only reach up to her elbow. Damn! How could she know my intentions? After several weeks of skating with this doll, I laid it on the line. She had been skating with another boy as well and I needed her to decide between us men. I asked her who she preferred: me or Derek. She thought for a second and then said, "Derek buys me nice stuff, but you're more handsomer." It was a draw.

THAT SPRING I HUNG AROUND a bunch of tougher kids, hoping for some fun and adventure. A school buddy, whom I'll call the Mule, brought over a couple of blasting caps, which are used to set off dynamite. He had found them by his house when his street was being dug up to put in a newfangled water main. Since the town sat on muskeg over solid granite, dynamite was needed to blast a ditch to hold the pipe.

The Mule showed me a blasting cap and said his friend Victor had set one off and it'd made a huge bang. Cool! Excitement for once in this sleepy mining town. Three of us kids huddled around the explosive, our faces inches away from it, sheltering the tender flame from the breeze. Funnily enough, the electric wires attached to the thing just sort of melted; they didn't sparkle like the fuses in cartoons on TV.

The other kids got bored with the dud and eventually went home. Not being the type to give up so easily, I wanted to figure out why that baby didn't blow up. I took the blasting cap into our garage and pinned it in the vise my dad had bolted onto his workbench. Then I took a hammer and hit it a couple of times to soften it up. Eventually I got the little copper firecracker open to expose a light green powder inside.

Hmmm, that's gunpowder, I thought. *Better light this stuff up.* I carried the opened blasting cap, being careful not to lose any powder, outside to a pile of plywood that Dad had covered with a thick canvas tarpaulin (he was building a house at the time, something he did to keep himself busy). The stack of plywood provided a good surface for ignition, far from prying eyes, kind of like the steel tower used to suspend the atom bomb during testing in the Nevada desert prior to the actual incineration of Hiroshima in 1945.

I placed the blasting cap on top of the plywood, exposing the gunpowder, then giggled to myself as I noticed a neighbour gardening a couple of doors down, imagining that the huge bang would make him crap his drawers. I took my wooden matches, struck one against the side of the box, and watched the flame come to life. I glanced over my shoulder once more at the gardening neighbour. *This is going to be so funny*, I was thinking.

I stood back and gently tossed the match onto the green pow — *BANG! Holy fuck!* The cloud of exploding green powder launched me into another dimension, and the image is still stamped in my mind's eye today. I was blown back, my body ploughing a trench in the mud. When I sat up, my hearing was gone. The explosion had deafened me worse than any screaming episode from Chereyl.

I broke suction from the mud, picked myself up, and was turning to walk away when I noticed the neighbour staring at me in disbelief (and probably tugging at the seat of his jeans to pull out denim that had been swallowed by his sphincter). Brenda's hand-me-down orange terrycloth T-shirt was full of holes. Blood was running down my arms and dripping from my hands.

Trying to act like nothing happened, I stumbled to the back door of the house, where my Dad and Chereyl were standing. Dad had his hand over his mouth in shock, mumbling, "Oh God, oh God."

Blood was streaming down my face, and I shook my head to fling it out of my eyes. Chereyl kept saying, "What a stupid kid. What a stupid kid." (It made the CBC National News. I can't remember how they actually announced it, but to my ears it sounded like "Stupid Kid Blows Himself Up in Geraldton!") The blast had blown a hole in the tarp and created a crater in the plywood stack.

Dad drove me to the hospital in the station wagon while I wiped off the blood as best I could with a wet facecloth. The doctor said I was lucky, that someone must be looking out for me. The last person the doc had worked on who'd had an accident with a blasting cap had lost several fingers. I kept all of mine.

The only casualty was the fingernail on my middle finger, which was split in two. I kept trying to swipe what looked like hair out of my eyes but never managed to get it out of the way. The doctor said I was bleeding inside my eyes from the concussion of the blast. (I'm sure I would have lost my sight completely if the cap had blown when we three kids were huddled around it, just inches away.) My face, chest, and arms were covered in tiny burns; I now looked like an eleven-year-old with a bad case of acne and track marks from heroin abuse. The whites of my eyes had tiny burns too, like pepper shaken on a fried egg, and I had pieces of copper embedded in my chest that the doctor just left in.

I went to school the following Monday morning wearing Brenda's sunglasses because my eyes were still very sensitive to light, which suited me just fine because they were oversized aviators that hid most of my face. After morning recess, we kids filed into Mr. Kuneman's grade five classroom. On the end of the row of bookshelves at the front of the room was a cool-looking puzzle box. David White and I checked it out briefly and then sat down at our desks. After all the kids were settled, Mr. Kuneman asked David and me to stand in front of the class. We were a quite a sight: David, who was miraculously even shorter than I was, and me by his side with my sunglasses, acne, and track marks.

"These boys are dead," Mr. Kuneman stated, which was quite a shock to me. "Only two people opened that box at the end of the bookcase: David and Bryan. What if that were a bomb? Luckily, it's not. David, sit down."

David gladly sat down. I was squirming by now and feeling nauseated, what with my stupid-looking sunglasses, the weeping sores on my face, and the regret I was feeling for not wearing my sister's pants that day and having to stand in front of the class wearing floods. I stood there as Mr. Kuneman went on and on about how lucky I was not to have been killed, and for the other kids to look at my sorry state to remind them to be careful in the future.

Grade five was a pivotal year for me. I was getting my stride as the class clown and hell-bent on being a famous person. My confidence was growing and I chased my dream of becoming a professional hockey player. I knew the names of all the hockey greats of the day, but my favourite was Bobby Orr. Number four for the Boston Bruins. I picked up his book from the library and read everything about him. Bobby Orr was born in Parry Sound, Ontario — a small town like Geraldton. If he could become a famous hockey star there was, in my mind, no reason why I couldn't become famous too.

I read that many famous hockey players used to practise every morning before school on ice rinks their dads had made in the backyard. We didn't have a rink.

But I needed to put in the effort of training if I wanted to be a famous hockey player on television. One night, after deciding I would do anything it took to be a hockey great, I slept in my clothes, woke up at four in the morning, laced on my skates, grabbed my ninety-nine-cent stick taped just like Bobby Orr's, and skated across the road to the ice rink in the neighbour's backyard.

I did my own impromptu skating drills and took some shots with a puck I found in the snowbank. I didn't stay long. I was still sleepy and was freezing my ass off.

After a couple of minutes I skated back home and found my dad at the back door of our house. He was frantic having thought I was sleepwalking and would freeze to death. He wasn't mad. Just relieved. This is what you have to do to be a professional hockey player, I told him. That week Dad made our own rink.

I practised skating every day for hours and shooting pucks at a bucket sunk in the snowbank to improve my accuracy. I played street hockey with the bigger kids to challenge my abilities. My parents were concerned about me playing with kids five or six years older than me and double my size, but I didn't mind the occasional bump or being the butt of an off-colour joke. This was the price to pay for stardom.

We didn't play with a plastic street hockey ball like kids do today because typically at twenty below zero, which was a normal winter day in Geraldton, the ball would freeze hard as a rock leaving welts on your legs where you got hit. And me being the smallest kid would be the recipient of many welts because the boys usually had me playing net because I was the slowest. We occasionally bought a soft hockey puck to use but they cost nineteen cents and if we lost it, it would be a while before we had enough money to buy another one. In that case we kids would ball up the paper packing from a crate of mandarin oranges and wrap up the ball in electrical tape. It was black like a puck (for visibility in the snow) and didn't leave a mark when you stopped a shot. We only got mandarins around Christmas time so we had to make several "pucks" to last all winter until the warmer months arrived.

For my sixth birthday Mom and Dad got me a hockey helmet. I was in heaven. Dad enrolled me into organized hockey and I soon became one of the better players for my age group. I loved it. I played hard, but because I was still one of the smaller kids I got hurt occasionally.

One morning after a hockey game I woke with a headache. I didn't want to tell anyone because I just assumed everyone got headaches. Magazines were filled with ads for headache medication.

Over the course of the day, my head began to pound. I couldn't pay attention to what was going on in class. Concerned, Mr. Kuneman came over to me. I told him that I had a headache and he suggested I put my head down on my desk and sleep if I can. I appreciated being singled out. All the other kids in class had to work on their assignment but I got special treatment. I liked being special.

Everyone knew that Mr. Kuneman was an avid canoeist and outdoorsman because he drove to school in a baby-blue Ford pickup truck with a camper on the back. Geraldton was an outdoorsman's paradise: the town was surrounded by lakes, with great hunting, fishing, and canoeing within arm's reach. For years Mr. Kuneman took students with him on camping trips. Usually, one or two boys at a time.

I enjoyed camping and on hot summer nights I used to sleep in a tent Dad had set up in our backyard. I loved the solitude of reading comic books and having my own hideaway. That spring of 1974 Mr. Kuneman asked me and my two buddies — we three sat together goofing off and trying to amuse others around us — to go on an overnight camping trip with him. We were excited. I just hoped my parents, being strict as they were, would loosen their leash on me a bit and let me go. I told my parents that kids had been going on canoe trips with Mr. Kuneman for years. They saw nothing wrong with it. Cool!

He picked up us three boys in his baby-blue Ford and drove to an isolated lake a few miles down one of the many lumber camp roads that surrounded Geraldton.

It was just an overnight trip, but we learned a lot. Mr. Kuneman taught us how to use the J-stroke to paddle a canoe properly and how to make a campfire even if the wood was wet, both essential skills if you live in Northwestern Ontario. After a long day of canoeing the three of us kids had a great time roasting hot dogs and marshmallows and got to joke around with immunity in front of our teacher.

A couple of weeks later, the three of us were to go on another canoe trip with Mr. Kuneman. He pulled up to my house and I waved to Mom, grabbed my pack, and went out to the baby-blue camper truck. But, only one of my two friends was coming on this trip. Maybe the other kid was sick, I thought.

After a damp, cold day of canoeing, the two of us and Mr. Kuneman converged in the camper to have dinner, tell jokes, and read comic books. My classmate and I were to sleep on the upper bunk and Mr. Kuneman was to sleep on a bunk made by lowering the dining table. Once we were ready for bed, we decided to roast marshmallows on the gas stove. My classmate and I took those long-pronged tools used for barbecuing and roasted a couple of marshmallows, igniting them and holding them up like Olympic torches. We posed for photos. It was a fun trip.

The following Monday, my classmate and I met up with the other kid who missed the trip and asked him why he hadn't come out with us. He said his mother wouldn't let him go. I wondered why. He had pretty cool parents who let him do a heck of a lot more than mine did. It seemed odd to me.

Over the winter there were no camping trips, but when I played hockey at the arena, Mr. Kuneman would come and watch, standing in the bleachers by himself. He was always by himself. He never seemed to socialize with other adults.

I was invited to his place once. Mr. Kuneman's house was on the old mine townsite, and when I entered I was confronted with stacks of yellow Kodak boxes of slide carousels on his living room floor. I remember thinking that, yes, he was a photographer and that was probably normal for a dude with a camera. He said he had managed a rock-and-roll band of young boys back in the day and showed me a picture of the group while playing a recording of them doing a Beatles tune. Even though I remember thinking they weren't very good, they were only a couple of years older than me, and I thought it was pretty cool to be in a band at thirteen.

Spring came late the next year and Mr. Kuneman asked me once again to go camping with him. My other buddies weren't asked, so I went on the trip by myself. I think it was just for one night and I don't recall anything other than fishing and canoeing. But I do remember our drive on our way back to town the next morning. Mr. Kuneman asked me if I wanted to stop on the way home and go tubing down some rapids.

I thought, *It's too cold to go swimming, dumbass!* But I said I couldn't go because I didn't have a bathing suit.

Mr. Kuneman said, "You can just go in your underwear ... or no underwear at all."

Red flags popped up inside my eleven-year-old head. Panicking and wanting to jump out of the truck, I pressed myself against the passenger window. But I held it together and said casually, "It's too cold."

"Suit yourself. Maybe next time," he replied.

The following week at school seemed really strange. I carried a sick feeling in my stomach and I couldn't look anyone in the eye. With a sense of dread, I was thinking, *what have I done?* I felt like a criminal. Mom asked me why I was so quiet. I said I had a headache or something like that and retreated to my bedroom.

That weekend I was to go on another trip with Mr. Kuneman. I told my mother I didn't want to go camping with him. Of course she asked why. I just told her that I didn't like camping anymore, that there were too many mosquitoes.

I knew what time he was to pick me up, so I hid in the bush and watched his baby-blue camper stop in front of my house. He got out and knocked on the door. Mom let him in and he was inside for forty-five minutes. I knelt in the woods, frozen with fear, until he got back inside his truck and drove off. My hands were shaking and my knees were throbbing from kneeling in the wet undergrowth.

I'm sure he wanted to confront me at school in the days that followed, but I purposely distanced myself, hanging out with my friends so I was never alone. Eventually he went camping with another boy. Seeing them drive through town, I copied the "cool" kids and started labelling any boy who went into that baby-blue camper one of "Kuney's boys." Deep inside, I felt sorry for them. Even as an eleven-year-old boy unfamiliar with human sexuality, I knew the difference between a homosexual and Mr. Kuneman. Homosexuals were nice people who smiled; I called them "fairies," because fairies were always friendly and kind to you. Mr. Kuneman was a *fag*. Dirty — like the British slang for a cigarette. Gross and dirty. (Writing about this episode forty years later, I know that such language is abhorrent and I feel horrible about using these words, but as an eleven-year-old that was the only terminology to which I had been exposed.)

One night, decades later, I was watching a movie with my wife when the phone rang. I didn't recognize the number and picked up the receiver. The Blind River division of the Ontario Provincial Police were calling. The first thing that popped into my mind when I heard who was on the line was that the call was to inform me that a family member had been killed in a traffic accident on some provincial highway. My heart began to pound like a phonebook bouncing around inside a dryer as I spoke to the detective, not really hearing his words the first time he spoke them.

"Do you remember a man by the name of Narcisse Kuneman?"

"Who?" I said.

"Narcisse Kuneman. He was a teacher in Geraldton in 1974?"

"Oh yeah. Why do you ask?" I was relieved not to be hearing about the vehicular death of a family member.

"He's been arrested on charges of child molestation and after searching his premises, we found pictures of you. We also found his journal, which had, for lack of a better word, a hit list of young boys, which you were on."

"Yeah. I thought something like that might come up. Where can we talk?" I asked.

I met the two detectives at a hotel on the airport strip in Toronto.

They informed me that Mr. Kuneman, my grade five teacher, had been arrested for touching a boy inappropriately after the boys' parents had hired him as a tutor to teach the shy boy street smarts. When he got home, the boy told his father that Mr. Kuneman had touched him in a bad way, and the father, instead of beating up the man who'd molested his child, went to the police. Based on this report, the police in Blind River, where Kuneman was living and taking care of his aging mother, searched his residence and found forty pairs of boys' briefs and a couple of hundred photos on his computer hard drive. That's where I came into the investigation.

Flash back to 1974. We all thought Mr. Kuneman was a great teacher. In retrospect, he was so good at teaching that when he tutored that particular young lad to watch out for bad people, it backfired on him. I liked him a lot except for the time he embarrassed me by having me stand in front of the class, the victim of a blasting cap accident. He had always had a passion for art and photography, and it was the photography that ended up being his undoing. He took photos of everything. And everyone. He journalized and kept lists as an obsessive-compulsive would.

Fast-forward to about twenty years later, as the detective showed me photos of myself taken inside Kuneman's camper. There was the one of my friend and me in our underwear, smiles on our faces, holding up our flaming marshmallows. Another picture showed me in the camper in my underwear flexing my abs. Mr. Kuneman would often show me photos in muscle magazines, and as a kid I always wanted to be a muscle man.

"Can you do that?" he would ask. I could, crunching my little abs as he snapped a photo.

The detective asked if I was wearing Kuneman's underwear, because my pair looked too big for me.

"Hell no! My parents bought my clothes two or three sizes too big so I could grow into them."

The trial that led to Mr. Kuneman's demise started with the hit list. One of the kids affected, now an adult, was tracked down in prison. When the detectives asked for his help in the case against Kuneman, he basically told the cops to shove it. Considering that he was in jail, I imagine that he wasn't too fond of the police. Then the detectives told him he could remain silent and allow Kuneman to abuse other boys, or he could stop it now. The former victim bravely agreed to cooperate. He matched names from the journal to the photos taken as evidence. He was the one who identified me.

The detectives showed me scores of pictures of my classmates posing in compromising positions while covering up their private parts. Kuneman had journalized everything. One of the detectives read me an entry, without revealing the boy's name, in which Kuneman described him as "gaining weight nicely." That grossed me out. They read me a couple of descriptions of acts that need not be repeated. I was shown pictures and I identified several boys I had looked up to and wanted to emulate, boys I had played hockey with. Now, as an adult, my admiration for those boys has not changed.

I was one of the lucky ones. I was one that got away. Fifteen other boys were not so lucky.

AFTER I STOPPED CAMPING WITH Kuneman that spring, I devoted my time to kids my own age and shared laughs and mischief with my two buddies from his class. In an act of rebellion, after school we often stole cigarettes from our parents and hiked deep into the woods to smoke them.

Close to us there was a confectionary store that the three of us used to frequent. The owner was an older gentleman who we all thought was about a hundred years old, but was probably in his sixties. In the summer months he would close the store from two to four in the afternoon.

One summer day the three of us walked into the store around three o'clock. No one was around. It dawned on us that the store was closed but the door wasn't locked! Wow! We could rob this place. As we cased the joint we decided that we would just do it and keep our mouths shut. We each grabbed a handful of shoestring liquorice and bolted. But, not before one of my buddies grabbed a pack of cigarettes and matches.

We hightailed it out into the bush and gobbled down our liquorice and smoked the entire pack of cigarettes. It was at that point we wondered why we had talked ourselves into doing such a stupid thing. We could have been caught by the police and thrown in jail! But the real regret was because none of us were smokers and killing twenty butts made us three very sick boys.

I trudged home and went to bed. Mom came in to tell me that dinner was ready. I told her I wasn't hungry. I felt sick. She knew exactly what I was up to. She smiled. "Serves you right."

After learning our lesson from our crime spree, the three of us decided to pursue a more healthy choice in lifestyle. One of my buddies had a set of weights his dad bought complete with a pamphlet selling a bodybuilding course. It showed pictures of Dave Draper and Arnold Schwarzenegger, Lou Ferrigno and Frank Zane. All stars from the golden age of bodybuilding. There also was a photo of Mr. Canada next to a lake posing and flexing by gripping a paddle. I flexed my bicep, looked at the tiny bump, and declared then and there that I was going to be Mr. Canada one day.

We were lifting weights on my friend's lawn, flexing with our shirts off and tanning, when we noticed a column of black smoke in the woods across the road. We put our shirts on and ran down a path that was a snowmobiling trail in the winter until we got to the fire. A makeshift log cabin, probably built by teenagers so they could have a place to drink, was in flames. The surrounding brush was burning as well. The three of us grabbed sticks and began beating the flames back. An older boy named David came running down the trail. He told us he had made a fire but put it out. Sirens were approaching from a distance and we told him to take off before the police got there. We wouldn't say anything.

Firefighters from the volunteer fire department arrived and began dragging hose into the woods to extinguish the flames. The first firefighter asked me if we started the fire. We told him the truth: we saw the smoke from my friend's house and came to put it out.

Our faces were blackened from the smoke and we were exhausted from our frantic efforts to beat back the flames, but all three of us had beaming smiles. "We're heroes," I said to the other two. "Maybe they'll put our picture in the paper." It sure felt good.

5

Escaping a Terrible Fate

I CONTINUED TO THREATEN MY existence on a daily basis in my preteen years, as I considered myself quite the daredevil. Evel Knievel was a huge star at the time. I had just seen a live broadcast of his aborted attempt to fly across the Snake River Canyon in a rocket-powered motorcycle.

I had hungered for attention all my life, and I figured if some redneck could become famous for doing stupid shit then I could pull off a brainiac stunt in dramatic fashion as well. I was too young for a grownup motorcycle like the one Knievel used, and my parents refused to buy me a minibike because money was tight and food was more important to the family than my glory. So I decided I would have to do an equally terrifying stunt (for the wow factor) on my old "pop-a-wheelie" bicycle.

Bisecting the town was a little river we called Shit Creek — my own Snake River Canyon. It was about fifteen feet wide with a ditch about ten feet deep. Since the water at the bottom of the ditch was only eight inches deep and full of old tires and shopping buggies, I would be sure to kill myself if my jump fell short. Definitely good for the wow factor.

I would have to build a ramp to launch my bike over the Shit Creek gorge, so I asked my dad if he would build me two ramps, one for take-off and one for landing on the other side.

"No," he said.

"How about just a launch ramp then?" I could land on the rocks and maybe blow a tire or break an arm, but it would still look great.

"No."

"Okay, forget about ramps. Can I borrow a couple of planks and a cement block or two?" I was hoping he wouldn't figure out that I was planning to construct a makeshift ramp for the jump on my own.

"NO!" Dad had figured it out. Damn.

Dejected, I went to my buddy Lennard's house to hang out for a bit. Across the street from him was a pink house where Donald, a boy a little younger than me, lived. His parents were super-strict and wouldn't let him out of the yard to play cops and robbers and stuff with us. From the vantage point of my buddy's place, I could see that this oppressed young man had been bitten by the Evel Knievel bug as well.

A load of gravel had been dumped next to Donald's house (I guess his dad was going to make cement shoes or something for the family). I saw Donald fashion a ramp out of the gravel with a shovel and then get on his bicycle. I figured he was going to jump the fence, much like Steve McQueen did in *The Great Escape*, giving his henpecking parents the finger as he soared over the barricade to freedom.

He eyed the ramp for a second or two, then started pedalling towards it like a bat out of hell, hitting the ramp at probably twenty miles per hour, sending him into the air. I should clarify: the *kid* went into the air while the bike hugged the pile of gravel. Our next-door daredevil was still holding on to the handlebars as he hung upside down for a second, then descended at rapid speed, mashing his nuts on the crossbar of the bicycle. Donald crumpled as the bike cartwheeled and crashed into the chicken-wire fence, ripping open his nose. At the precise moment when his face smashed into the fence, I looked into his eyes and we connected on a sort of cerebral, telepathic wavelength. *Don't do this*, he seemed to be saying. I decided that the daredevil life was not for me.

THE YEAR I TURNED SIXTEEN and got my driver's licence, some school friends were working for the Ontario Ministry of Natural Resources as junior forest rangers during the summer. The job entailed cutting brush and making firebreaks around small communities in the province. Older kids — they had to be at least eighteen and had finished school — worked on the forest firefighting crews. They got paid a good bundle for slugging hose and eating mosquitoes for weeks at a time.

The provincial government had set up forest fire–fighting stations around Ontario. Since Geraldton was part of the James Bay Frontier, right in the middle of the bush, it stands to reason that fires would burn in the forests around the town. My dad worked as the groundskeeper, facilities manager, gofer, and all-around custodian of the Ministry's air base, just outside of town; he was lucky to get the gig after the mines closed. One of the jobs he performed was driving the fire gear, pumps, hose, and whatnot up to the fire camps when forest fire season started. There were always fires burning throughout the province every summer, unless it was an unusually wet and depressing one.

At the end of the summer Dad got to take home all the unused (read: uneaten) canned goods. This was the only time we had awesome things like Jell-O pudding in the house. We kids prayed for a summer of few fires, not because we were averse to the idea of the town being consumed by a firestorm, but because we would get fruit cocktail cups for lunch.

ONE MORNING LATE IN THE season (August 22, 1979, to be precise), I was walking to work in town when I saw the Ministry bus taking my friends with the junior ranger jobs to their last day of work before school started up again. I wanted to be with them, but the Ministry of Natural Resources had a nepotism clause: no family members were allowed to work together. So, I had spent the summer doing odd jobs.

I waved to my friends, wishing Dad could have gotten a job somewhere else so I could have been on that bus and making the big coin. I walked home for lunch that day and was cooking up a can of soup we'd scrounged from last year's fire season when Dad came in.

"Something bad's happened. The radio's going crazy."

I asked him what had happened and he said he didn't know.

After the soup and fruit cocktail, I went back to work. As I was walking home after I'd finished for the day, the town had a strange pall over it. Dad was talking to Mom when I walked in the door.

"Seven people dead," he said to me.

"Jesus, what happened?"

"Doing a prescribed burn. Got caught inside," he said, with his head down. "Terrible screaming. Terrible."

A prescribed burn rids the forest of dead and diseased trees so there's less fuel for a potential forest fire. The year after a burn, new saplings are planted to regenerate the woods. To execute a prescribed burn, a fire is set in a large U shape. As the fire burns towards the middle, the top of the U is lit and the fire burns against itself, clearing an area for future planting. It's dangerous work that requires two or more crews working in tandem.

What went wrong in this case, the inquest revealed, was that the top of the U had been lit before the crews had got out from inside it, trapping eight people. The supervisor, realizing what was happening, ran through the flames, getting severely burned before jumping into a pond. He pleaded with the others to run through the flames to the pond but they, all teenagers, didn't follow his example and perished. Four of them were good friends of mine whom I had waved to that morning on the bus: Ken Harkes, seventeen; Colleen Campbell, sixteen; Wanda Parise, sixteen; and Andy Thompson, sixteen. The seven kids were found in a pile, the boys on top, trying to shield the girls from the fire — a last act of gallant bravery for these young men. The disaster became known as the Esnagami Lake Tragedy.

The town was numb. A group of classmates converged at someone's house that evening and we just looked at each other in disbelief. All of us shed tears. That feeling of invincibility I had as a sixteen-year-old was shattered. What if I had been one of those kids on the bus? Had I cheated death again?

6

I Still Want to Be a Firefighter

IN MY TEENS DURING THE 1970S, I faithfully watched a TV show called *Emergency!* about Los Angeles County firefighters. But I didn't watch the show the way most kids did on regular TV. The only channel we got in Geraldton was CBC, but even though they were the national broadcaster and the most powerful television network in the country, CBC still got all snowy when a Ski-Doo drove by. Since my French-Canadian neighbours were members of the Geraldton Ski-Doo club, we missed a lot of shows in the winter.

Fortunately, if you were a subscriber to the Geraldton Cable Company, you got to watch a lot of the TV shows that people in the big cities such as the Lakehead and North Bay watched, because all the best shows were being bootlegged by said company. We subscribed. As it was explained to me (by a kid who said he was a spy from the Canadian Department of Heritage and Toboggans), the programs were recorded in California and then mailed to Geraldton and broadcast for the whole town to enjoy. The only downside was that the shows were about a week old, so the city folk got the scoop on what was happening on *The Young and the*

Restless before we did, a shame we young hockey players had to endure while playing in the larger urban centres.

I once got a chance to sneak into the secret dungeon of the Geraldton Cable Company. It was actually Colleen Emman's basement — her father was the entire company. I had accompanied my friend Laura Charr, whom I had a bit of a crush on, to her friend Colleen's basement to see the inner workings of a real live television station. I thought it would look a lot like the Bat Cave, with blinking lights and a nuclear reactor reaching up from the centre of the earth, complete with jets of steam shooting out of the granite walls of a natural cave formed within the Canadian Shield. It wasn't. Just a couple of cables attached to a Betamax.

A broadcast staple at TV Geraldton was the nightly Kinsmen bingo game. The elaborate set, also in the Emmans' basement, consisted of an ancient bingo machine (which had been hijacked from the parish hall) sitting on a table in front of a bedsheet hanging from the ceiling joists. A representative of the Kinsmen would draw a number each night and nuns and widows across town would check their cards, hoping to win a coveted prize such as a can of peanuts or a crocheted poodle toilet-roll cover. It was broadcast in black-and-white, of course, even though colour TV had been out for a decade or so. Viewers at home had to mute the sound because the bingo machine was so loud the speaker on the TV would rattle.

As I looked around the "studio," Laura said to me, "If you ever see the station go snowy and it's in the summer, it's because it's me doing this." And with that she pushed the eject button on the Betamax. I sat in amazement as the tape popped up from the top of the machine and the monitor next to it went snowy. Wow, what power!

IT WAS BECAUSE OF THE Geraldton Cable Company's bootlegs that I was able to watch *Emergency!*, a hit show by producer Jack Webb. Webb had made just about the only good television shows back in the day, *Dragnet* and *Adam-12*. *Emergency!* was a spinoff of those two shows and followed the day-to-day lives of two firefighter paramedics, John Gage and Roy Desoto, played by Kevin Tighe and a guy with the coolest name ever, Randolph Mantooth.

The show was exciting and gave a young gaffer like me a look into life outside my insular little world in Northwestern Ontario. All I could hope to achieve when I became an adult (unabashedly reinforced by my high school guidance counsellor) was to be either a mechanic, a welder, or a lumberjack, all of which sounded more or less like the occupation of every two-legged man in town (the one-legged men worked for the railway).

I once did an aptitude test to see which career would suit me. The results were pencil fixer, bone crusher, and tugboat captain (absolutely true story — I couldn't make this stuff up). Since I didn't like boats much and had no idea what a pencil fixer or bone crusher was, I deduced that I was on my own when it came to deciding a career path.

By this time, I'd realized that my career as a professional hockey player wasn't going to happen — I was too small and wasn't good enough. So I turned to a more secure occupation to pursue: rock star.

I worked every day after school and on Saturdays at a department store cleaning floors, taking out the garbage, and delivering furniture with Mr. Waylan, a retired musician who used to play on the radio in Winnipeg with the Happy Gang. I got $2.35 an hour and $7 for each furniture delivery. I was making as much as $500 on a good month. I would then go to Marino Hardware, my brother-in-law's store, to buy the equipment for a career in rock stardom.

God bless the Marino brothers, because I could order any top-of-the-line guitar or amplifier at cost plus 10 percent and put it on credit. At sixteen years old I had about $10,000 (manufacturer's suggested retail price) worth of music stuff. After I got my paycheque from the Hudson's Bay Company, I would walk across the

street to put some money down on my account. The cheque might
be for $238.49 and I would tell my brother-in-law (who became
the fire chief in Geraldton), "Hey, John, give me eight bucks back."
I was a good credit risk.

With all this music equipment, four of my likeminded buddies
and I formed a band called THRUST! (Or, as one venue printed
on a ticket, THURST!) Four guys, four chords — there was no stopping us now. My quest for rock stardom had begun.

I figured I was done with school. I wanted to tour full-time with
THRUST!/THURST! but my parents wouldn't let me quit. And if
I quit I wouldn't be allowed to use Dad's pickup truck to move
our band stuff to gigs.

School was now just getting in the way of my music. On one
high school report card, for my typing class — essential now, but
back then it was just an easy credit, and if you were lucky you
got to sit next to a girl with big boobs — the teacher wrote: "Bryan
constantly disrupts the class endlessly talking about his rock band
to anyone who will listen." Clearly, I thought, she didn't know
I was going to be rich and famous and she would someday be
giving interviews to documentary filmmakers, saying things like
"I knew him back when" and "He was such a nice boy."

A woman who worked upstairs at the department store I worked
at had a son who was a musician and sound engineer at Le Studio
in Quebec. His pay was so poor he was basically starving, but one
of the jobs he had at the studio was to pick up the musicians from
the airport. His mother told me he had just picked up the Rolling
Stones for a recording session. That was good enough for me.
The Rolling Stones! They weren't worthy to lick KISS's platform
boots, but they were at least sort of famous among the older kids.
I decided then and there: I wasn't going to be a rock star. I was
going to be to be a music engineer for a recording studio, working
with bands like Teenage Head, Rush, and April Wine. But how?

In high school my electronics teacher, Mr. Wyse, was an
inspiration for me. He saw something in me I didn't see myself,

which was either an underlying confidence or benevolent cockiness (whichever you prefer). With his coaxing, I decided to apply myself and go to college for electronics, a surefire ticket to the recording studio. Fortunately, in my last year of high school, I won a bursary to pursue a career in electronics based on his recommendation to the school board. The bursary was sponsored by Marino Hardware. I had a hundred bucks to blow on an education in electronics! Mr. Wyse is gone now; he passed away a couple of years after I moved to the city. He died much too young — victim of a hereditary heart condition — and I still miss him.

Off to Toronto I went, but the joy was soon taken out of learning. It took about a week for me to realize that electronic engineering is hard stuff: it's all about calculating base current and crap like that. I sucked at it — math is not the strong suit of this gifted artist — and I didn't pay attention in class. As I stared out the window of the classroom, I would watch the fire trucks go by, sirens wailing, weaving in and out of traffic. *Hey*, I thought, *I'd like to do that!*

So, when my professor scolded me once too often for day dreaming during class, I said, "stick the math up your ass, I'm going to be a fireman," and walked out. I went straight to the El Mocambo, the legendary club where April Wine recorded a live album with that sort of famous band the Rolling Stones (who co-headlined as the Cockroaches), to drink myself stupid while plotting my future career as a firefighter.

With the help of a monetary lifeline from my dad, I took every course I could think of to better my chances of getting into the fire department. I got my first aid certificate, jogged up and down the stairs in my apartment building to get myself in shape for the physical testing, and bought a book from the World's Biggest Bookstore — *Essential Vocabulary for the College-Bound Student* — for the written exam. Ironically I was no longer college-bound, but the purveyor, a corpulent curmudgeon, fervently endorsed the treatise.

7

The Next Chapter

A FEW MONTHS AFTER I moved to Toronto in 1981 to attend college, my high school sweetheart, Lise, dumped me. We'd talked constantly on the phone and she'd visited me once, but she wasn't interested in a long distance relationship and had no intention of moving to Toronto away from Geraldton and her family. I was heartbroken. Crushed like any eighteen-year-old who had mourned a four-year relationship would be. I was never one to play the field and casually date. I'm what you would call a serial monogamist, dating someone until I get dumped then immediately searching for another girlfriend.

While searching for another girlfriend, I learned electronics is not the curriculum you want to study if you want females in your class with whom to socialize. All my classes were filled with guys. There were a couple of young women in a couple of my classes, but they were all spoken for.

Heartbroken and homesick, I called home every day. The phone bills used up all the money I had saved for a trip, so during the summer break I stayed in Toronto. My two sisters Chereyl and Brenda were my daily counsellors trying to keep my spirits up and encourage me to stay positive. Chereyl and her husband John, a Geraldton volunteer firefighter, allowed me to call daily and reverse the charges. I can't imagine how much it cost them in telephone long distance charges to keep this heartbroken boy from packing everything up and moving back to Geraldton defeated.

In school I had made a couple of good friends who were, like me, from small towns. We were all missing our hometowns and high school friends. One of my new friends, Paul, from the Maritimes, invited me to a party in Brampton. As I had nothing else going on, I went with him.

The party was a small affair with a few students drinking and listening to music. Paul had a girlfriend, Michelle, whom he'd met while commuting to school and she brought her best friend along. Her name was Linda.

As the night went on the four of us went for a walk. Paul and Michelle decided to go back to the party while Linda and I kept walking. She seemed nice enough, and she was smart. She was going to start nursing school in Toronto in the fall.

We walked for a bit until we discovered we were lost. I was totally out of my comfort zone. Geraldton was a small town. Even if you could get lost in Geraldton you just had to keep walking to eventually hit the lake, the tracks, the bush, or Main Street.

But Brampton is not small, and Bramalea, the subdivision we were lost in, was a series of crescents and cul de sacs that left me dizzy. To make matters worse, each section of Bramalea had streets whose names all began with the same letter of the alphabet. The section we were in, as I recall, was "G." How many street names can you think of that start with "G"? There are quite a few, as it turns out, and it took about an hour for Linda and me to finally find the right street and make our way back to the party. In the interim we got to know each other and even managed to smooch a bit. I was homesick and heartbroken and Linda seemed nice. We began to date.

As I waited for replies from the fire departments I'd applied to, I moved back home to Geraldton for the summer months to work and save some money. My brother-in-law's family owned an amethyst mine about a two-hour drive outside of town and they hired me for the summer to be a miner and general labourer. I drove a dump truck and bulldozer, repairing the road leading into the mine site. The job gave me valuable practice driving heavy equipment. While at the mine site, I lived in a small, beat-up trailer with a portable radio and guitar to keep me amused. My reading hobby was satisfied the day I found a box of *Reader's Digest* volumes stuffed in a cabinet under the sink. They were of consecutive months from 1948 to 1952. Colourful ads posed questions like, "What will the new 1949 Buick look like?" or confirmed for every man that all he needed to do to please a lady was to buy her a Brand New Proctor Automatic Toaster.

Linda moved to Geraldton for the summer to be with me, staying at Chereyl's house and getting a job at Marino Hardware: my brother-in-law's family store. Mom didn't like Linda much. "She's got you under her thumb," she would say.

Dad just wanted to see me happy but didn't want me to become a firefighter. "Too many dead people" he would say. Later, I would find out that he was right.

After a week of working at the mine I drove back to Geraldton on the weekends to score some good home-cooked meals and to spend time with Linda. On one Saturday morning at the mine site I gobbled down my breakfast of bacon and eggs and bolted out the door of my trailer to drive back to town, leaving my dirty dishes in the sink. I came back to the mine on the following Sunday night to find the windows smashed on the trailer. The door was ripped off its hinges. Upon entry I discovered the inside completely trashed. Mud, dish soap, and peanut butter covering every inch of the trailer. My bed was torn apart. The culprit wasn't a human, though; a bear had been drawn by the smell of my greasy dishes and had broken into the trailer. There were teeth marks in my guitar case, the dish soap bottle, the peanut butter jar, and the sugar container. The bear, I believe, felt trapped and broke through the window over my bed, leaving bits of fur on the shards of glass.

At the end of the mining season I packed up my clothes from the patched-up trailer, picked up my Fender guitar case with the teeth marks in it, and drove back down the mine road for the last time.

My brother-in-law John was a member of the Geraldton Volunteer Fire Department and for a few weeks in the fall of 1984, convinced the chief, Danny Koroscil, to let me practise with the fire crew, wearing SCBA (self-contained breathing apparatus) and performing drills to see if I felt confident I could do the job of a firefighter. I loved it. Chief Koroscil wrote a letter of recommendation for me to supplement the fire department job applications I was submitting.

I moved back to our apartment just off Yonge Street in downtown Toronto. Still in pursuit of a firefighter job, I trained for the physical testing by running up and down the stairs in my twenty-storey building. A few times a week I walked to the Toronto Reference Library a couple of blocks up Yonge to research Toronto Fire Department annual reports, hoping to get an inside scoop on the fire department that I could capitalize on during the testing process. The Toronto Fire Department was incorporated in 1874 and in 1984, the City of Toronto was celebrating its sesquicentennial. A 150 year anniversary Memorial Volume was published which I pored over constantly. In the fall of 1984, the Toronto Fire Department had a recruitment drive.

I rode the streetcar to write the exam at the Toronto Fire Academy. I wasn't sure which stop to go to and asked the driver if he could tell me where to get off for the fire academy. He looked at me. "You're too young to be a firefighter."

"I'm twenty-one," I said. He let me off at the same stop where, coincidentally, thirty-one years later, while struggling with the mental stress of being a firefighter, I was to come across a fatal motorcycle accident on my way to work.

The exam session was one of several the academy was conducting; there were four thousand applicants for only thirty-five positions. When I arrived at the fire academy, dozens of men and a few women were queuing on the front steps, waiting for their opportunity to beat the odds and win the coveted position of probationary firefighter. We were led into the auditorium where row upon row of desks were set up for the exams. The exam consisted of tests for basic mathematics and English and a series of drawings of gears, wheels, and levers for mechanical aptitude. At the beginning of the session a training officer read a number of facts about a series of streets and buildings, reading off road closures and traffic and weather conditions. The scenario went on for a few minutes, with the officer counting off the number and locations of hydrants in the area, the number of railway crossings and what times a train came through. Then we would have to answer a number of questions based on the facts we'd been given, testing our ability to digest information. I looked around the room at the dozens of applicants hunkered down writing the exam. All wanted the same job I was after. I believe that in life you make your own luck and at that moment in my mind I was going to make myself the luckiest guy in the room.

A month later I received a letter stating I had advanced to the physical testing round. I was going back to the academy.

When I arrived I found a series of testing stations set up inside the fire academy training tower. My adrenaline was pumping. I could smell the smoke from the gear.

The first station was a blackout maze to test if you were claustrophobic. A training officer spewed a series of instructions, but in my nervous state, the only words that stuck out were "We'll fail you if you remove the facepiece." The rest of his instructions were a blur. I donned my blacked-out facepiece and was led into a room. *What did he tell me to do?* I managed to remember that the man had told me get into a crawling position to enter the chamber. *Shit. It's a chamber? What did he say about a chamber? I can't remember!* I crawled inside and immediately came to a dead end. *What did he say?!* Feeling around with my hands I felt all sides of the chamber. It was a tunnel about three feet high. To my left was a chair or stool. I couldn't get around it. My instinct was to pull off the mask and see what the hell I was dealing with, but I remembered the only instruction the officer told me. "We'll fail you if you remove the facepiece." There was no way they were going to beat me. I felt around, looking for a way past this obstacle, then realized I could crawl underneath. I continued to crawl down the tunnel and came to another dead end. Using my hands again, I could feel that I was blocked from the front. A wall. On my right was another wall. *The opening must be on the left.* Again, I was blocked by a wall. *What did he say?* I reached above me and found open space. I climbed up to the second level and continued moving forward, pushing things out of my way so I could pass until I came to another dead end. At this point I was comfortable in the chamber and went through my routine of reaching up and down, left and right. Then I heard the officer's voice again: "Take off the facepiece." I removed it, my face moist from perspiration, and took in my surroundings. I crawled out of the chamber and stood up to face my inanimate foe. The chamber was a metal maze with a series of windows on one side. If I had snuck a peek when I was behind the first obstacle the training officer would have had a clear view and I would have failed.

Back in the training tower a ladder was set up to the fifth floor to test applicants for a fear of heights. This time I listened to the instructions intently. *Climb to the fifth floor. Enter the window. Climb back out and down the ladder to meet me here.* Got it. As I climbed up the Bangor ladder it bounced. The aluminum rungs were freezing. I had never been up a ladder that tall and I was terrified. My knuckles were white from gripping the rungs. Going up was terrifying but I made it to the fifth-floor window and jumped inside as I'd been instructed. A training officer inside asked if I was okay. I lied and said it was no problem. But now I had to climb out on the ledge five stories up and get back on the ladder to climb back down to the apparatus floor. In my head I was saying *Just do it. You'll fail if you don't. Just do it.* I held my breath and climbed out onto the ledge. Nobody was going to stop me. Nobody. I made it down safely. I continued the rest of the testing with little problem. The butterflies in my stomach were gone and now I felt I could really do this job.

After about a year of applying to every fire department within a subway ride, I got the call. I was to report to the Toronto Fire Academy on January 7, 1985. The Toronto Fire Department wanted me on their roster.

8

Learning the Ropes

I WAS A BUNDLE OF nerves on the first day of drill school, but I was excited to start a real career other than the pencil-fixing or bone-crushing gig my guidance counsellor's aptitude test had me pegged for. The chief of the job stood in front of us and welcomed us to the TFD — 150 years of tradition unimpeded by progress. He said his only regret was that there was an empty seat up front for a new recruit who couldn't, for family reasons, join the class. He went on to say that this new recruit was a well-known professional football player for the Ottawa Rough Riders of the Canadian Football League, Maurice Doyle. All the guys in the class nodded in recognition of the star. Being the artsy type rather than a sports guy, I played along. "Maurice Doyle. Yeah, a big black guy, right?" I said, playing the odds. Nope. He started his career with Toronto in the next recruit class. A few years later I did end up working with Moe on several fires. He's a good friend and first-class guy in every respect. His son is now a firefighter with Toronto Fire.

A man from the Republic of China was also in our class on an exchange program. His English was limited and my Chinese was a bit rusty, so our communications were a tad strained. No worries. The chief explained how progressive the Toronto Fire Department would be and went on to introduce another recruit: Peter Chow, a Canadian-born man of Chinese descent.

The chief got both of them up in front of the class and had the two firefighters greet each other, a hands-across-the-ocean kind of thing. Great photo op. Flashbulbs flashed. The two men smiled and said a few words to each other — and that's when we discovered they spoke completely different dialects. The uncomfortable silence ground away at our bones as the tender moment crashed and burned.

After the chief had finished his speech, a guy from the firefighters' credit union showed up. He told us to sign up to start having our paycheques deposited in the special financial institution run by the brothers. "Get yourself a loan, kid. They aren't going to fire you if you owe the city money," he advised.

I soon had awesome job security. Funny, the first thing they told us about being a firefighter — as opposed to a fire*man*, which is a person who shovels coal on trains — was how great the benefits and pension were. Benefits? Hmmm ... Cool fire hats and boots. Ring the bell. Slide down the pole. I got it. I leaned over to the guy next to me and asked what a pension was. "Don't get married" was all he said.

In 1985, the fire department in Toronto was run in a very military fashion. The upper echelon were all veterans of the Korean War. They were tough as nails, and they wanted the men on the TFD to be just as tough as they were. That didn't bode well for me. I was young and excited — but very young. The first fire truck that I drove on the training ground was a backbone of the TFD, a 1954 American LaFrance pumper. Ten years older than I was. Don't they have a newer truck for me to learn on?

Like little soldiers we froze our asses off on the training ground, raising ladders, dragging hose, reloading the hose we had just pulled off the truck, and my favourite, spraying water from the top of the ladder one hundred feet in the air. The wind would blow the water back in your face, filling your boots and eventually turning you into a Popsicle.

It turned out that years of training for cold weather by playing road hockey in Geraldton doesn't mean shit when you're soaked to your underwear and dragging hose around. Standing frozen as a cigar-store Indian, I asked my tough-as-nails instructor through chattering teeth if I could sit in the truck during a fire to stay warm. That was a source of guffaws on the job for years.

My class of thirty green recruits was split up into groups according to height. Think about that for a second. If you have four guys of different heights carrying a very heavy ladder, the tall dudes will be bearing the brunt of the weight and the little guys will dangle underneath like laundry on a clothesline. I was in the Smurf group.

We drove 1950s LaFrance ladder trucks, or aerials, as they're called in Toronto. They were the same fire trucks they used in Los Angeles ... in the 1950s. They also had California cabs, meaning there was no roof over the driver and crew. They were built like that, according to the 1950s owner's manual, so when we pulled up to a hotel or skyscraper fire, the driver could see up above and get a better idea of where to position the truck for rescue operations. I get the whole rescue thing, but I still found that design feature puzzling; February in Canada is a tad cool to be cruising in a convertible with the lid down. I'm no automotive engineer, but I'd definitely throw in a roof and maybe a heater.

Another point about the "California Cooler" missed by the sharp minds in the TFD's purchasing department was that during a fire, dozens of hose lines are deployed by gorilla men and the fire is put out with — wait for it — water. Thousands of gallons of water. It would have been nice to have a roof on the truck to keep the seats dry. During those cold Canadian Februaries, water that fell in the cab would turn to — wait for it again — ice! (We learned this from the Popsicle exercise.) Not only do you end up exhausted from dragging hose and smashing walls, when you return to the truck you have to take an axe to the steering wheel to break off the ice so you can drive the hunk of frozen rust home.

ANOTHER PURCHASING DEPARTMENT BRAINSTORM OCCURRED during the late 1990s. Toronto used to be a busy shipping port for everything from sugar and rubber to tractors. In 1965 the city had purchased a new fireboat, the *William Lyon Mackenzie*. It could pump more water than ten fire trucks and had a snorkel basket that rose fifty feet above the water, where it could be used as a vantage point for firefighting and rescue operations alongside large ships. It could pump foam to fight oil and fuel fires, had a galley for the crew with enough provisions for several days away from port, and a hospital bed for emergency medical care during an incident. It was even a Coast Guard–certified icebreaker that kept the shipping lanes open for the ferry that was used by the people who lived on Toronto Island year-round.

The *William Lyon Mackenzie* served the city well and earned a place in the history books as an essential part of Toronto's firefighting arsenal. But in the nineties, its increasingly expensive upkeep and the drying up of ocean-going shipping traffic meant that its days were numbered. Although the city still needed a fireboat for the buildings on the island, the *Mackenzie* seemed like an albatross. The incoming fire chief made a decision to replace the ageing craft, and the purchasing department issued a tender for two smaller and lighter quick-attack fireboats.

To much fanfare, a contract was made with a company from Vancouver that specialized in aluminum watercraft. The price was exceptional, jobs would be kept in Canada, and the new boats' performance would blow away the dinosaur now docked at the marine fire station — a win-win-win scenario. In those tough economic times, the city could potentially save millions with the lighter boats, which, unlike the *Mackenzie*, didn't need a large crew and expensive upkeep. Heck, the annual cost savings were so huge they even bandied around the idea of buying a third boat.

Months later, the light-attack boats were built and the customizing of each craft began. As items from the marine firefighting crew's wish list rolled in, the special additions added to the original cost of the project. Slowly the costs rose. Cool fire-engine red paint. Emergency lights? Yeah, top-of-the-line! Hydraulic hoist? Of course! What rescue boat didn't have one? Sonar, GPS, and top-notch radio communications? Hell, yeah, throw in the whole package! Motors?

Wait, no motors? Christ, no wonder they were so cheap. Again, I'm no engineering wizard, but I would've asked for motors ... just for that whole mobility thing.

The bosses did their best to keep this blunder under wraps, but with firefighters being the overgrown children they are, it didn't take long for it to get out. A prankster jumped on the news. (Let's call him "Anybody But Me.") In short order an ad was placed in *The Boat Trader*: "Eighty-foot icebreaker for sale. Fish finder. Sleeps one. Cherry-picker basket. Like new. Six thousand dollars, or will trade for two light-attack boats." It used the chief's name and home address too — pretty funny stuff. (Note: Lawyers have no sense of humour.)

EVERY DAY AT THE FIRE academy was like day camp. We worked hard studying hydraulics and building codes as well as medical instruction in the classroom. But the real fun was during the live fire training. With my fire gear on I almost felt like Superman. Indestructible. Nothing could hurt me.

Then the instructor showed our class of recruits a film about the potential dangers of firefighting. He said, "If you change your mind about being a firefighter after seeing the film, there's no shame in that."

The lights dimmed. The projector rolled and the recruits sat back to watch.

One of the first scenes showed a fire in a propane plant in the 1960s. A large body of fire was consuming a propane tank the size of a railway car. The firefighters were standing their ground, pouring water on the flames, when one end of the tank blew out sending the massive cylinder across the yard like a rocket. Several firefighters were mowed down by the cylinder, while the fireball from the explosion swept across others, evocative of the Hindenburg disaster when men fled the flaming dirigible only to be cut down by the fire.

Another scene showed happy firefighters on the back of a pumper, waving to the camera as they race to a fire at a construction site. When they arrive a moment later, a dynamite shed on site blows up. The film shows the fireball and subsequent destruction, while playing the audio of the radio transmission from the incoming chief: "Dispatch, send a couple of ambulances. There's been a massive explosion. It blew the windshield out of our car... and we're a quarter mile away."

The class was quiet. There was some stirring among us young eager recruits, but it was clear to all: This is a dangerous job. I no longer felt indestructible. I felt vulnerable. The images of that film, seen over thirty years ago, are still fresh in my mind and remind me of how fortunate I was to come out in one piece.

9

Riding the Rigs for the First Time

MY FIRST POSTING AS A recruit was to a fire hall downtown in a trendy area known as Yorkville. In the 1960s Yorkville was a hot spot for the Canadian hippy movement, with coffee shops frequented by musicians and future icons, like Neil Young, John Kay of Steppenwolf, and Jimi Hendrix. By the 1980s the cafes were long gone, replaced by upscale shops catering to the wealthy and upwardly mobile.

Linda and I were living in an apartment building a few blocks south of the Yorkville Fire Hall and conveniently only a couple of blocks from the hospital Linda was working at. I was nervous about being posted to such a busy fire district. We as recruits had endured several weeks in the classroom, and now for our final component of firefighter training we were stationed with real fire-fighting crews. We were still on probation and could be sacked at any time if we weren't up to the task. I knew I would have to function clear-headed in a dangerous environment and have to deal with dead and dying people. Would I be able to cut it?

I packed my fire gear into a bundle with my boots, coat, and helmet strapped together with a belt. I gave Linda a kiss goodbye

on that spring afternoon and left my apartment to walk to the
fire hall and start my first night shift on an active fire truck. In
the hallway a woman stood next to me while we waited for the
elevator. I was feeling so proud of myself. *Look at me. I'm a real
firefighter.* She stared at me for a second then down at the bundle
of gear; helmet strapped atop with rubber boots sandwiching a
canvas fire coat.

"Fencing, right?" she said.

"No," I told her, feeling a bit deflated, "I'm a firefighter."

"Isn't that a volunteer thing?" I told her firefighting was my full-
time job.

"What, even in the winter?"

I got to the fire hall unsure what I was supposed to do and
introduced myself to the captains and firefighters having coffee in
the kitchen at the back of the hall behind the apparatus bay. One
of the captains said, "Throw your stuff on the pump." I stepped
back out to the apparatus floor to the pumper truck. I didn't know
which side to place my fire gear so I put it on the back step and
stood beside it for a few seconds looking kind of stupid until one
of the firefighters welcomed me into the kitchen for a coffee. I
learned having a coffee at the change of shift was the normal daily
routine of fire crews across the city. The night crew had a coffee
and gabbed to each other about the calls they'd had overnight and
the incoming day crew gabbed with the night crew asking them
about the same calls. At the afternoon change of shift the day crews
updated the incoming night crews about rumours on the job and
new department memos, and the night crews were glad they weren't
working the day shift.

The Yorkville Fire Hall was a beautiful building built in 1878 for
the Village of Yorkville Fire Department and annexed with Toronto
in 1883. The men working at the hall told a story of how when
the station was renovated in 1974, the interior walls of the hose
tower were removed to reveal hundreds of antique liquor bottles that had been dropped between the joists from firefighters

drinking in the tower decades ago. I giggled, picturing firefighters from the 1800s partying on duty at the top of the clock tower. I was told in no uncertain terms that they weren't "partying." They were "self-medicating." Years later I would understand the term self-medicating first-hand.

I met the other recruits from my class that were posted there. They said they had a busy day and passed on a few tips they had learned from the veteran firefighters about how to arrange my gear and position the trucks when they backed into the bays. Me, as the fifth wheel, would shadow the real firefighters, stay out of the way, and try not to get anyone killed. The unlucky captain assigned to babysit me was a hard-core firefighter affectionately known as "Hump the Grump."

On the night shift I learned that I had to check my equipment to make sure it was ready to respond to an emergency and study my manuals and notes while I waited for said emergencies. The other recruit I was posted with, Peter Stairs, was a couple of years older than me and a much better student. I wasn't very good at note-taking and Peter had a detailed series of index cards filled with facts. *I think I'm out of my league.* Peter was assigned to the aerial and I was to run with the pump for this shift. Hours dragged by while we waited for our first real emergency, the anxiety eating away at both of us. My mind wandered, refusing to ingest the information on the pages of text in front of me. Seven hours went by without a single call. A visiting captain having dinner in Yorkville parked at the hall and came in to say thanks for the use of the parking lot. Hump the Grump told him about the lull in call volume and the visitor said, "That's got to be some kind of a record for you." I knew it. I was cursed.

An hour or so later, the alarm rang. "Pumper ten respond to the report of smoke coming from a vacant house." I bolted to the fire pole, sliding down with lightning speed, then ran to the pumper and strapped on my gear. I hung on as the truck, lights flashing and siren wailing, weaved through traffic until we stopped in front of an old Victorian home at #5 Lowther Street. It was dark outside and there were no lights on inside the boarded-up home, but I could see faint wisps of smoke against the streetlights. My heart was pounding in my chest.

We pried back the plywood covering the front door. Inside we discovered an older man standing next to a metal pail with a small fire in it. He had been using the fire for heat. My captain told him we would have to extinguish his fire. The man didn't want the police involved. "Go get a hand pump," my captain said to me. I rushed outside and didn't know what compartment contained the hand pump — a water can with rubber hose and manual pump. I knew I needed an extinguisher, so I grabbed the first one I saw; A CO_2 extinguisher used for electrical fires. I brought it inside to put out the fire, and when Hump saw I had the wrong piece of equipment he told me to forget it. He called on the radio for the driver to bring the proper extinguisher. I felt stupid. Hump told me not to worry about it — there would be plenty of opportunities to redeem myself. I wondered how many strikes I would be allowed before they fired me.

On my first day shift we had a call for an electrical fire in the rear of a restaurant. The joint was just a couple of doors down the block from the hall; we arrived while I was still getting my equipment strapped on. The crew jumped off the truck and went inside to investigate. I was slow to get ready, but at least now I knew which cabinet had the CO_2 extinguisher in it.

Hump the Grump emerged from inside the restaurant, and in his big, booming voice yelled, "Get me a handline!" A fire! My first real fire! I barked at the pump operator that we needed a handline. He put the truck into pump gear, jumped out, and grabbed a quick-attack handline. I packed on hose and marched up to the door, nozzle on the left shoulder, pile of hose on the right.

Hump the Grump really grumped when he saw how expertly I was hauling the thirty feet of fire hose. He shouted, "What the hell are you doing? I wanted a hand *lamp*!" I decided then and there that if I ever got to become chief, it was going to be called a flash-light. Strike two.

MY FIRST REAL FIRE AS a recruit took place in a frat house on the University of Toronto campus. Hump the Grump was on my tail, shouting the entire time, "Get the kid in there! Get the kid in there!"

Getting ready to "get in there," I hauled the hose line and humped it up to the second floor of the big old house. Flames were licking out from underneath the door right in front of me. The guys set me up in front with the charged hose line as one of the older guys smashed in the door. The room was engulfed in flames. I panned it with the powerful stream of water from my hose. It was all over in a couple of minutes, and there I was, standing in the middle of a burnt-out bedroom. Was I a hero yet? It sure felt like it. "You did good, kid," said Hump.

The place was packed with blackened clothes, charred pizza boxes, and a large assortment of glass jars containing a bubbling liquid. It had got hot enough during the fire that whatever was in the jars had reached its boiling point. I guessed he had been bulk shopping, being a frugal student and all that. I opened one of the larger jars and took a whiff. Piss! The guy was so goddamned lazy he couldn't walk the six feet down the hallway to use the wash-room! Probably a techie millionaire now. Loser.

LATER, DURING MY TENURE AS a rookie at the Yorkville station, we had to deal with a very smoky fire in a five-storey apartment building that was started by a plumber using a torch to repair some water pipes. It was burning in the walls and spreading through-out the century-old building. The walls were the original lath and plaster, filled with horsehair and sawdust for insulation — perfect fuel for a smouldering fire. There was a lot of smoke throughout the entire building, but the flames had yet to break out.

The lights left on in the smoky apartment looked like headlights in the fog. Several times I thought I had found the elusive fire, but no, it was just a light. They'd never told me about that in firefighting school. How am I supposed to find the fire if I can't see it? So there I was standing in a smoky empty apartment with no fire to put out.

Not knowing what else to do, I went for a piss. I played to the decorum of the room, standing at the toilet and breathing through my mask as I peed. *Ring, ring, ring!* Was my air running out? *Just what I need*, I thought, *to be found dead in my first big fire, out of air, with my pants around my ankles.*

I checked the gauge and I still had lots of air. I pulled up my pants. *Ring, ring, ring!* It wasn't the gauge — the phone was ringing. *Shit, nobody's home.*

"HELLO?" I shouted through my facepiece.

"Is Diane home?" the female voice asked. I'm sure she was wondering what the hell Darth Vader was doing at her friend's place.

"No, she's not at home right now. Try her at work," I said, doing my best to be helpful.

"Who is this?" she demanded.

To which I replied, "The fire department. Her place is on fire. Have a good day." *Click!*

10

My First Fire Death

AS A RECRUIT SHADOWING THE firefighters at the Yorkville Fire Hall I became aware of the number of fire deaths they had dealt with in the past. I wasn't eager to experience the gory stuff the vets were joking about at the breakfast table.

In the Yorkville running area is a development called St. James Town: a series of nineteen high-rises built in the 1960s of between fourteen and thirty-two stories in height. With a population of approximately seventeen thousand people it was the most densely populated square mile in North America when they were built.

I was working a night shift on Pumper 10 when the call came through to the hall for "alarm bells ringing" at 375 Bleecker Street. We arrived at the building. No smoke was showing upon arrival. The alarm panel indicated a pull station was activated on the twenty-fourth floor. Our crew arrived on the floor and could smell smoke, but again, none was visible. There was a fire somewhere. The radio crackled. Dispatch was now saying there were alarms activated on the nineteenth floor. We lumbered down the stairs, then one of the trucks radioed that they had a working fire in an apartment on the tenth floor. We humped our equipment down

the stairwell as quick as we could. Smoke was pushing into the
stairwell and I started to mask up as we got to the tenth floor.
A firefighter from within the apartment pulled out a burned body
and dropped it at my feet. My heart jumped. The captain immediately called for an ambulance to the stairwell. I looked at the body.
The clothes were burned off. It was a woman. Skin was hanging
from her arms. Her face was black from smoke. My hands shook
as I strapped on my facepiece and turned on my air. I crawled into
the smoke to back up the firefighters inside. I gulped air from my
mask as I tried to concentrate on the fire in front of me.

Back at the fire hall I went over the ordeal in my mind. Could
we have saved that woman if we were sent to the right floor at
the beginning? The tenant on the twenty-fourth floor had smelled
smoke and pulled the fire alarm, just like you're supposed to, but
no one had pulled the alarm on the tenth floor, where the fire
was actually located.

Back at the fire hall the next morning as the day shift came on
duty, we read the morning paper and found a story with details
on the fire. The deceased woman was in her eighties. Neighbours
said she often lit a candle for her husband, who had passed away
recently. It was surmised that she had again lit a candle and that
her nightgown had caught fire.

The day shift firefighters asked about the fire. My captain told
them his recruit — me — had seen his first fire death. "Not a bad
one," he said. "Just some skin hanging off." But to me, it was a
bad one. You always remember the first one. Vividly.

Finishing Up My Training

BY THIS TIME LINDA AND I were doing really well. The financial pressure was easing with both of us, she as a nurse and I as a firefighter, making decent wages compared to when we were students skimping to get by on part-time jobs.

One sunny Sunday afternoon that year in June, Linda was working a day shift at the hospital. I had been working night shift, so I was sleeping until after noon when I was awakened by music coming from down the block. I was still tired, but the music was too loud to allow me to sleep any longer. Maybe I should check it out. I walked from my apartment building down Dundonald Street to Church Street. Balloons and banners were strung across the intersection. It was definitely a block party. A stage had been set up and a band was playing "You're Having My Baby" while a chorus line of men was doing a cancan routine. People were having a great time and I welcomed the opportunity to decompress after a busy night of running alarm calls. The sun was shining, and most men had taken their shirts off. *Great. I could use a tan.* I was preparing for my first bodybuilding competition and was quite muscular and lean. I pulled off my T-shirt to soak up some rays and show off my hard-earned muscularity a bit. I blended into the crowd of shirtless partiers to watch the band and have fun. Then this naive small-town boy realized he was enjoying no ordinary street party. This was my first Pride Day. Vive la différence!

I GOT INTO THE SWING of things as far as studying went and after several fires under my belt, my confidence and abilities had progressed to the point where the crews were relying on me like I was one of their own. After a few weeks I had mastered driving the fire truck through the crowded streets of downtown Toronto. My captain, teaching me to fly through the gears on the manual shift pumper, had me drive around Queen's Park Crescent, the street surrounding the site of the provincial legislature. Hump had me drive the pump south on University Avenue coming from north of Queen's Park, upshifting to build up some speed. As we rounded the legislature I downshifted to decelerate and turned left around the curve to merge with the northbound traffic. Again, we picked up speed northbound past the park on the north side of the legislature merging left to begin our way south again and start the circuit over again. Our fire truck did this circuit over and over again, accelerating, decelerating, circling the provincial legislature again and again. The crew sitting on the back of the pumper were probably sick from going around in circles for a half hour or so. By this time, the Provincial Police assigned to the legislature were watching us with suspicion. The crew on the back would wave to them as we made each pass. Turns out Hump had me learn on the best "track" a young firefighter could ever want. The rest of my probationary period at the Yorkville Fire Hall went without a hitch.

THE RECRUIT GRADUATION CEREMONIES AT the fire academy ran in tandem with the Rescue and Station Citation Awards for the rank and file firefighters and were well attended by family and friends. It was great to catch up with the rest of my recruit classmates, most of whom I hadn't seen since I left the academy, to share stories of fires and station anecdotes.

As we lined up to enter the auditorium one of my classmates commented on a group of teenage girls fawning over a young man with huge spiked hair wearing a sports coat with the sleeves rolled up to the elbow. "What's the deal with Rod Stewart over there?"

"That's my brother," said Greg Steffler, a classmate of mine. "Rod Stewart" was Chris Steffler, the drummer of the hugely successful pop band Platinum Blonde.

We marched in under Pipe and Drum wheeling in through the crowd and sat down at the front of the auditorium. Our recruit class had practised marching on parade for the weeks we spent at the academy prior to being stationed for our probationary period and filed in crisp and clean. The firefighters after spending years on the trucks and out of marching practice stumbled in mis-turning and out of step to the chuckles of a few. My family didn't make the drive to Toronto for my graduation, but Linda was in the audience to witness me receiving my uniform hat and badge. It was the proudest day of my life.

12

My First Posting

IN ADDITION TO GRADUATION CEREMONIES, the fire academy is used by recruits, rank-and-file firefighters getting recertified on equipment, and firefighters rehabbing injuries. On our last day of our fire academy training the posting came out for the recruits' permanent station assignments and I heard my name called.

"Who's Ratushniak? Who's the rat?"

"That's me!" I said.

"I know where you're being posted," said the guy, who had a handlebar moustache. We all knew from the war stories that the old guys — the guys with handlebar moustaches — had been through the shit and knew where the action was, which was right in the city core. Older stations with low numbers like 1 or 3 or 5 or 7 or even 10, the Yorkville station I trained at — busy and crazy.

"You're going to 29," Moustache quipped. A high number. *Very funny. Really? Shit.* "Your captain's crazy and your truck is on PIP." PIP is code for pre-fire inspection planning: drawing floor plans and checking standpipe hookups. And my captain was crazy?

Station 29 is in Forest Hill, a very affluent section of Toronto in an old-money way. The fire station used to be the village of Forest

Hill's town hall, complete with municipal offices, a fire station, and a police station. The prisoner cells were still in the basement of 29. The old Forest Hill guys used to tell stories of running the radio room for the police: when a fire call came in, they would run across to the other side of the building and jump on the fire trucks.

The City of Toronto annexed Forest Hill in the 1960s, so you can imagine how spunky those guys were in the late eighties, when I got there. All the "Forest Hillers" were really old and set in their ways: they ate the same stuff for lunch, parked in the same spots, and so on. With no more vacancies at the station, I was going to be the sole young pup for a while.

My first day on duty in my new hall was a gorgeous spring morning. I showed up early, the first guy on my shift to arrive. I went upstairs to meet the crew and was greeted by the night shift, who were having coffee. The sun shone through the kitchen window, which was on the second floor over the apparatus bays. There was Moustache sitting on the windowsill, sipping his java. Smiles all around.

"Hey, young fella, welcome to the hall." *This will be okay. Everyone is so nice.* I grabbed a cup from the selection of mismatched coffee mugs, poured some joe, and went to sit at the large wooden kitchen table that is the cultural nucleus of every fire station. This was going to be all right — good coffee, friendly crew. I sat down at the table and everything stopped dead. I think in the background I could hear tires squeal and a record scratch.

All eyes glared at me. What had I done? "That's Jimmy's seat," one of the geezers said. So I moved over one seat. Still the cold stare. Two seats over, I planted my ass again. Safe. Birds continued in flight. The earth began to rotate on its axis again as if nothing had happened. *Gee, can't wait till I meet my crazy captain.*

My crazy captain was a guy who looked like Johnny Carson, but with a prizewinning comb-over. The first words out of his mouth were "Welcome to the hall." Then he went on to say that he was the smartest man he'd ever known.

In the kitchen there was a large blackboard used for training purposes, but it was also a repository for notes and a list of canteen supplies the hall needed. Once a week the winning lottery numbers were scribbled dead centre on the blackboard (for dramatic effect, I guess). Each time, when the numbers went up, my captain would look at them and impress us with his mathematical acumen. Say the numbers were 3, 6, 12, 21, 32, and 49.

"Oh, look, it's the magic sixes!" he would declare, then take a piece of chalk and show us why we were all so stupid not to pick up on that. "Three, that's easy. That's half of six. Six is of course six. Twelve is two times six." For emphasis he would underline the number six every time he made this deduction. "Twenty-one is twelve backwards, which is two times six." *Underline.* "Thirty-two: if you add the numbers three and two together, they equal five, which is one less than ... that's right, six. And of course forty-nine, which is seven squared, which is written as seven with a little two. So if you add seven plus that little two, it comes out to nine, which is six (*underline*) plus three, which is one half of six." Wow, how could I have missed that?

Being the new guy on the truck, I would be the driver for a while. My job was to drive the truck and operate the pump at fires while the old guys got to do the glory work, rescuing orphans and nuns and cats and stuff as I stood outside. After the equipment was checked and I was given an orientation to the hall — "There's the phone, bed, toilet, and truck" — we saddled up and went out on our daily pre-fire inspection planning duties, checking the neighbourhood for firetraps. This was the land of Bimmers and Bentleys, though, so there weren't a lot of firetraps around.

While the rest of the crew was out doing PIP, I was able to sit in the pumper and study street maps. Neighbourhood familiarization: a good skill to have. It comes in handy when people call to have the fire in their house put out. The radio in the cab of the truck crackled into life and I was dispatched to my first emergency call as operator of the truck. I checked the address quickly. Thankfully,

I knew where it was. Good. I brought the truck to life and revved the motor. The emergency lights were flashing, ready to respond. My ancient firefighting crew hobbled out of the building.

I jammed the truck into gear and we raced off to my first fire with 29. My captain (a.k.a. Mr. Excitable) was yelling the entire way. I looked at him. "Shut the hell up! I can't hear the radio!" Okay, I didn't actually say that. This was the man who was going to lead us into battle. I concentrated on trying not to run over anybody.

This inaugural emergency, on Holly Street, was the longest three minutes of my career. The captain screamed at me the entire way. "Slow down! Speed up! Left! Right! Watch the light post!" Just as we approached the address, I slowed down. He yelled, "Stop here!" as he punched me in the chest. Turns out there was no fire, just a maid who set off the fire alarm system by burning the non-fat, gluten-free vegan cookies she was baking for the mistress of the house.

I stewed the entire day, avoiding my captain and just studying my map book. I didn't want to screw up again. Wait a minute, I didn't screw up! I drove the truck in a safe manner and got to the address in a timely fashion. Yes, I was nervous, but who isn't on their first fire call? *Screw Johnny Carson!* I thought to myself.

I built up the courage to confront my captain, knocked on his door, and marched into his office. "You know, I can take constructive criticism," I said. "But I don't have to take your abuse. I don't appreciate you hitting me like that." He nodded.

Two minutes later we got another run. Sure that I was going to be fired for talking back to a superior officer, I figured I'd better enjoy my last fire call. I made that fire truck's tires squeal. Pedal to the metal, white knuckles all the way to the call. Mr. Excitable, eyes as wide as saucers, saw the demented expression on my face and seemed about to launch into a tirade. But instead of screaming at me (*Change lanes, asshole!*) he held his tongue and, with the restraint of a thousand horses, popped out his finger — *boink* — to point to the next lane. I didn't get fired.

BEHIND THE FIRE HALL IN Forest Hill was a telephone pole with a tin tulip nailed to the top of it. Once a year the aerial ladder truck was set up during our Sunday morning equipment check and someone painted the tulip. Apparently it had been up there for decades.

I asked one of the older guys, a Forest Hiller, why we painted this tin tulip. "A guy who worked here had a daughter who died a slow and painful death from cancer," he said.

She loved tulips, so, in his daughter's honour, this firefighter placed a tin flower he made at the top of the pole directly behind the station. It's perfectly framed when you look through the window from the kitchen upstairs. The man would sit and drink cup after cup of coffee while staring through the window at the tulip. Sometimes he would smile; sometimes he would cry. He's long since passed on.

MY CAPTAIN AT THE FOREST Hill fire hall took some getting used to, but my acting captain, a guy by the name of Robert Gray, was also a character. We called him Scotty because he had been born in Scotland. He had come over when he was a kid, so he didn't have an accent — until he was drinking, when he turned into Angus McCrock from SCTV. "Aye, ya wee 'un! Away wi' ya!"

He was also, to reinforce a stereotype, cheap. "Is anyone having soup for lunch?" he once asked. "I need a can to fix the exhaust pipe on my wagon." When he wasn't lamenting about the Highlands, he had a mouth that could make a biker blush. "So I was driving on the four-oh-fucking-one and this fucking truck with these huge fucking wheels almost fucking runs me over …" You get the idea.

In the days before the City of Toronto was amalgamated with its adjacent municipalities, the fire departments were completely separate. Station 29 was a border fire hall, so we occasionally ran into the City of York fire department's hood for emergency calls. It was a silly system if you think about it; the city had become one huge metropolitan area, and the only way you could tell you were stepping over the border into another municipality was that the fire hydrants were a different colour.

One day we had a call to an address on the border between York and Toronto. The York fire department was already on scene and waved us off.

Scotty got on the radio to inform dispatch of the situation. "Control, we've arrived. York Fire is already on scene and waved us off. We're going to fuck off back to the hall."

"Roger, Pumper 29 ... Call Chief 46 when you get back." I knew by the tone of the dispatcher's voice that our district chief, Chief 46, had heard the foul language over the radio. He was not a happy man on a good day. Scotty, I knew, was in for trouble.

"Roger, Control." Scotty turned to me and said, "I wonder what we fucking did now?"

I would not include excitability in a list of desirable attributes for a leader. We were all excited and anxious at emergency calls when we first started on the job, but after a couple of years most firefighters settle down and deal with emergencies in a controlled and professional manner. A few firefighters, for whatever reason, never seem to appear controlled at a scene. My captain at 29 was one such firefighter. On one occasion, we answered a call for a report of smoke in the hallway of a high-rise. Smoke means we need self-contained breathing apparatus, or SCBA. There are two ways of putting on an SCBA. One is to swing it over your shoulder and strap it on much as you would put on a knapsack. The second is called the overhead method: You grab the unit with both hands, tuck in your elbows through the straps, and lift, bringing the air cylinder up over your head. You drop it down and, voila, you're wearing an SCBA. I used the swing method because you can do it as you walk towards a building; my captain used the overhead method.

When we arrived, smoke was showing from a balcony. Naturally, Mr. Excitable bumped up his enthusiasm a notch. I jumped off the truck and trotted to the front door, swinging on my forty-pound mask as I ran. Mr. Excitable bent over, grabbed his unit, and attempted to fling it over his head. But it didn't quite make it. *Kloon!* — the bottom of the air cylinder smashed into his forehead. His comb-over stuck straight up like an off-centre mohawk. His eyes rolled around inside his noggin, and smack dab in the middle of his forehead you could see, for lack of a better term, an impression of the bottle's on/off valve. It was reading "off" at the time of impact.

Our crew quickly put out the burning trash on the balcony and ignored the frantic running about by our captain.

13

Spreading My Wings

BODYBUILDING HAS ALWAYS BEEN AN important part of my life. I admired the dedication of bodybuilders like Arnold Schwarzenegger and his best friend and training partner, Mr. Olympia Franco Columbu. But, I was also drawn to the artistry of classic physiques like that of Mr. Olympia Frank Zane.

I had been training daily at a gym around the corner from my apartment making great gains in muscularity and decided I was going to challenge myself to see if I was as good a bodybuilder as I thought I was. Having decided which would be the most entry-level of the entry-level bodybuilding competitions, I entered the Southern Ontario Novice Bodybuilding Championships in Niagara Falls. I didn't tell anyone at the fire station I was competing in case I bombed and came in last and they laughed at me.

I didn't realize there is a specific way to prepare the week leading up to a show. The food consumed during the final week is timed specifically to maximize muscle shape and size, and consists of a cycle of carbohydrate depletion and subsequent loading as well as limiting sodium and a final dehydration phase.

The night before my first competition, I worked the night shift on Pumper 29. We had few calls that night, which allowed me time, in the wee hours of the morning, to apply self-tanning lotion to my body, hoping to God no one would walk into the bathroom and catch me in my underwear covered in cream. In the morning after my shift, I picked up Linda from the apartment and set out for Niagara Falls.

I hadn't planned the drive carefully and it wasn't until I checked the map that morning that I realized the trip would take two and a half hours. I had to drive like mad just to make it to the weigh-in on time. I was flustered and nervous when I arrived. Everyone was in pretty good shape, many carrying a lot more muscle mass than me. At the judging phase of the competition we lined up in our respective weight classes on the stage, clad only in our posing briefs in front of a panel of judges and an auditorium filled with spectators. We performed the mandatory poses in unison to display the various muscle groups in comparison to each other. The judges scored according to muscle shape, size and conditioning, leanness, and symmetry (upper body in proportion with the lower body). Then each competitor went on stage one at a time to perform a posing routine set to music to display the muscularity in motion, each competitor accentuating their strengths and trying to hide their weaknesses.

My mind went blank once I stood on stage and saw the crowd. I forgot my choreography. I did my best to improvise a posing routine, throwing together a few poses and spinning around a bit, not really knowing what the heck I was doing. All the while my lip was stuck to my teeth in a creepy kind of smile because I was so dehydrated. But despite my off the cuff performance, I won second in my weight class and the Best Poser Award.

Back at work two nights later, I let the boys know about my foray into bodybuilding competition. Some of the crew were impressed, while one said I must be a "gearbox." All, however, were congratulatory.

By this time my six-month probation period had passed without any infractions and I was now a full-fledged firefighter. Linda and I had been together for almost four years and decided to make our relationship permanent.

Like the old Dean Martin song, I lived by the motto, "You're Nobody 'Til Somebody Loves You." She loved me.

Our wedding was planned for the following summer, with Linda's family flying in from England and my family driving to Toronto from Geraldton.

The travelling guests arrived Wednesday before the Saturday nuptials.

It was good to be with my family again. My brothers-in-law John and Donny took me out for drinks the night they came to the city. They, like me, were more comfortable with a casual evening of beer drinking and chicken wings than the white linen tablecloths and sparkling wine Linda and her family preferred.

I had one more shift at the fire hall the next morning before the Saturday wedding, then I was off on two weeks vacation. When I arrived for work at 29 I discovered my crazy captain had decided he couldn't mould me anymore. Like the others on my truck, I'd learned to ignore his tantrums and outbursts and he finally felt I was up to going out to relieve. Relief duty is a common part of the job. Each fire apparatus is staffed with an extra firefighter to accommodate personnel vacations, injury, and sick time. If all crew are on duty the extra firefighter is sent out to relieve on other apparatus that are short. That day I was assigned to Pumper 28, another truck in our district. When I arrived at the station I placed my gear on the pumper and upon sitting down to grab a coffee our truck was dispatched to a house fire.

Our truck was the first apparatus on scene. Smoke was puffing out a window on the first floor and I jumped into action to help the senior firefighter stretch a hose line to the front bedroom of a large house. The fire was confined to one room and we quickly knocked it down. The ceiling had fallen on the bed and contin-ued to smoulder as my crewmate sprayed water, trying to put out the last few flames. Another firefighter and I were to turn over the rubble-covered bed so the firefighter on the hose line could extinguish the burning mattress. I hoisted up the bed and began to push it to one side when I felt a pop in my back, accompanied by an immediate charge of immense pain. I dropped the bed and fell back. I couldn't move.

The others in the room helped me up. "I've screwed up my back," I told them. As I was in no immediate danger — the fire had been knocked down — they slowly walked me to the district chief's car so I could be driven to the hospital. I sat in the back seat of the station wagon, waiting for the chief and his aide to finish up at the fire. In my mind I was screaming at myself for ruining my future with a career-ending injury.

The chief dropped me off at Sunnybrook Hospital to get x-rays. After my examination, the doctor told me that I had torn a muscle on my tailbone. I'd be fine after a few weeks of taking it easy. I thanked him and hobbled to the waiting room for my ride back to work. A woman sitting across from me complained that I stunk of smoke. "Don't you guys shower?" Still wearing my fire boots and sweat-drenched fatigues and tired from fighting the fire, I didn't have it in me to tell her off.

My district chief picked me up a couple of hours later and drove me home to my apartment. I thanked him and told him I'd give him an update after I saw the fire department doctor. Linda, relieved my injury wasn't worse, met me at the door along with her young cousin, who was in town for the wedding.

THE WEDDING WAS A SMALL affair with fifty people in an old mill north of the city that had been turned into a luxury hotel. My back was still killing me, and I stood the minimum amount needed to make it through the ceremony. The next morning we flew to the Dominican Republic for our honeymoon. Fortunately, my rehab for my torn back muscle consisted of lying on a hot beach and floating in the ocean. Upon our return two weeks later, the fire department doctor cleared me to return to the trucks.

SOON AFTER RETURNING TO WORK, we received a call for an elderly lady who was having difficulty breathing. As a first-response unit, Pumper 29 answered calls for medical emergencies as well as fires, and we rushed to the woman's aid. When we arrived we found her on the floor leaning up against a chair, barely conscious.

The size of the home would be more accurately described in terms of acreage rather than square feet. The sitting room looked like something out of the movie *Sunset Boulevard*. It might have been Norma Desmond herself on the verge of croaking there. The only things missing were Max the butler and a dead monkey.

The place smelled of paint. Workers had been renovating one of the wings and I wondered if she'd become ill from the blue-collar fumes. Our captain wandered around the house looking for medication that might give a clue about this lady's condition, or at least a name on a piece of mail for the report in case she kicked off. I had been on the job for about a year at that point and, like the rest of the crew, just let Mr. Excitable do his own thing. It kept him out of our hair.

We knelt next to this aged woman of distinction. I put the oxygen case on the chair she was slumped against and applied a facepiece. She gasped for breath. As the oxygen made its way through her system, her colour came back and life filled her weeping eyes. She pawed at us and made a gurgling sound. I turned the oxygen up a little higher. She came around a bit more, until with a wet cackle she spat out, "Get that thing off my chair!" You're welcome, I'm sure.

The ambulance arrived just as she got her voice back and was giving us hell for not taking our boots off at the door. And how dare we touch her with our dirty hands, blah, blah, blah, how we'd dirtied her posh rug, blah, blah, blah, thirty-thousand-dollar antique, blah, blah, blah. We handed the bitch over to the ambulance crew and packed our stuff to leave.

Just then, the captain trotted past us and out the door. "Let's go!" he said.

We heard the old bag scream from the sitting room and turned to see what her problem was this time. Then we saw the captain's footprints — he'd tracked white paint across her rug.

By this point, I'd had enough. I wanted to get the hell out of Crazy Land.

14

From One Extreme to Another

I WANTED TO WORK AT a busier fire hall. I'd filled out several transfer sheets, trying to get relocated downtown, but Mr. Crazy kept ripping up my transfer sheets. "You don't want to go downtown," he said. I guess he thought it reflected badly on him when someone transferred out of his station. But the captain couldn't block me forever, and when he was on vacation, I found the opportunity I needed to sneak a transfer sheet out.

Not long after, the driver from the night shift came to me. "I've got good news and I've got bad news," he said. "The good news is you got your transfer. The bad news is you're going to 7."

Station 7 is in downtown Toronto. At the time it was the busiest fire hall in Canada. The place ran more than eleven thousand emergency calls a year that were handled by the three trucks in the hall: a pumper, an aerial ladder truck (to which I was posted), and a heavy rescue squad, one of two that covered the entire city. Each station is designated a number and the trucks housed there are numbered in accordance to the station number. Station 7 housed Pumper 7, Aerial 7, and 1 Rescue. The hall was situated in the middle of a part of town called Regent Park. The community was mostly low-rise apartment buildings and row housing, and was built in the 1950s as an experiment in social housing. It was a tough neighbourhood, filled with all the vices and problems that come with poverty.

My first ride out on the rig was for alarm bells ringing. I soon learned that alarms ringing didn't necessarily mean a fire — certainly not in that neighbourhood. It got to the point where we would, say, be reading a book in the dorm or working out and could hear the fire alarms ringing across the street from the fire hall. Knowing a dispatch would be coming in shortly we would automatically slide down the pole to the apparatus floor. Since it took about a minute for someone to call in to the fire department about the alarms ringing we'd have time to get to the trucks and put our gear on. By then dispatch would have processed the call and the emergency tones would finally have come through. The drug dealers in the Park kept us especially busy. A kid working as a lookout would pull an alarm to alert the crack house upstairs that the cops were coming. This would happen several times a night.

It was a stark contrast with Forest Hill, where the homeowners demanded we take off our boots at the door. In Regent Park we were grateful to have sturdy, waterproof boots whenever we found ourselves splashing around in urine puddles in the elevators. We would wear our gloves all the time because kids would rub shit on the door handles. We didn't dare touch the walls in case there were cockroaches who would climb on us — and you learned to shake out your coat before you got back on the truck. (Once the roaches are on you, they'll come back to the fire hall with you if you don't get rid of them.) Many of the people there lived like pigs, but half the cars in the parking lot were newer than anything I could afford. Go figure.

Because it was the busiest fire hall in the city, the pumper and heavy rescue trucks were fairly new apparatus, recently purchased to replace the worn-out rigs that used to run there. But the aerial was a California Cooler — just my luck. The month before I got there, a guy driving the new aerial truck had hit streetcar tracks at an intersection at just under the speed of sound, breaking the rear axle. It would be months before we got a new one. Great, and the winter months were just around the corner.

IN GENERAL, THE MORE BEAT up the fire hall, the more homey it felt. At least that was my experience. Nothing was new. It was all old. And not just old — beat up too. There was a time when the only way you got anything in the way of cups, dishes, or cutlery for the fire hall was when you had a fire in a restaurant. Things had a habit of showing up the day after a good fire. As you cleaned up the last of your eggs, you found yourself staring at the logo of the Golden Dragon Chinese food joint or some other condemned greasy spoon.

One score we managed on a regular basis was free ice cream from the factory on Poulette Street. My captain, Dan McMurray, was a schmoozer who always scored a case of Neapolitan (the stuff nobody liked).

The freezers in an ice-cream factory are cooled by somehow using ammonia (I don't know how; I'm not an engineer). So one day we got a call to the ice-cream factory for an ammonia leak. Cool! This was a chance to score some more free ice cream, and not that Neapolitan crap, either.

Ammonia calls are classified as hazardous material incidents. Ammonia fumes are lethal because they attack any moist parts of your body, and the insides of your lungs are very moist — they'll be burned by the chemical reaction in short order. Breathing apparatus is mandatory, and the rescue squad carried entry suits (encapsulating rubber suits) for that kind of thing. Before the suits arrived on the scene, if you needed to make a quick entry for a search — say, for a downed employee — you could create a makeshift moisture barrier by smearing your neck with Vaseline. However, we didn't carry Vaseline on the aerial ladder truck.

We arrived and the plant manager said all the employees were out and accounted for ... he thought. *Shit.* The guy's not sure. We had no way of telling how many possible victims were still inside. We couldn't wait for the squad to get there; they'd just cleared from a fire in the east end and were several minutes away. A person exposed to ammonia has only seconds before he will suffer permanent damage to his lungs, or even death. We had to go in.

Ammonia's effect on the body starts off slowly, as a warm sensation that quickly builds to a painful burn. It's similar to the gag we'd do as kids when we grabbed someone's arm tightly and twisted with both hands in opposite directions, causing a painful friction burn.

As we searched for employees who might or might not even be in the place, the heat was building up under our coats from carrying the heavy fire gear. The sweat was also building up. The moist skin on my neck was now burning, and then my armpits started to sting. The pain was unbelievable.

As my partner Mark and I got deeper into the building, the radio crackled. All the employees of the ice-cream plant were now accounted for. We had to get out. But we were sweating pretty good by then. *Christ, it burns! Got to get out! Shit, which way?* My neck was really burning now, and I could feel it spreading down my back. I instinctively crossed my arms to try to ease the pain in my armpits. *Got to get out!*

Now the sweat was rolling down my chest, burning all the way to my groin. Let me point out the obvious: the balls are located in your groin. My neck hurt — okay, I could handle that. My pits were burning — suck it up, no problem. But my balls? My balls felt as though someone had ripped them out through my pants and was working them over with a cheese grater.

But Mark and I still pressed on, joking about our "tender spots" for the rest of the day.

ON A GORGEOUS EVENING LATER that summer, we again expected to find multiple casualties when we answered a call for an explosion at a busy intersection in the city's core. The old, brick building was once a warehouse, but now housed a jewellery designer's shop. When we arrived on the scene, there was glass on the street from large windows on the second floor that had been blown out. Inside, we discovered the cause of the blast: the shop's power cleaner — a piece of equipment that puts jewellery under pressure to wash it — had exploded with enough force to fold the stainless steel sink it was sitting next to in half, while also blowing out a wall.

We got to the second floor and came across a man standing in the middle of the hallway. His hair was standing up wildly and his clothes were in shreds. He looked just like a guy in a cartoon who had held on to a stick of dynamite for too long. The poor dude was in rough shape, but it turned out he was one lucky guy — the steel sink had taken the brunt of the blast. Still, we asked him if he was okay.

"What?"

We asked again.

"What?!?!"

No kidding. The blast had temporarily deafened him. But then the man crumpled to the ground. He assured us he was all right, but shaken. We helped the fortunate man to walk to an ambulance.

When the power cleaner blew, all the gems sitting on the goldsmith's workbench had been caught in the blast, sending them onto the street below along with the shattered glass from the windows. Thousands of dollars' worth of diamonds, emeralds, and other precious stones were sitting in the middle of the street, mixed in with a couple of hundred pounds of glass shards. Several wheel-barrows full of broken glass with a handful of diamonds somewhere in the middle were swept up and locked away for one poor guy to separate. Glass ... diamond ... glass ... glass ... glass ...

15

Recruits Def: Pain in the Ass

JUST LIKE WHEN I WAS posted downtown as a recruit to learn
the ropes from the guys on the frontlines, we at Station 7 were
called upon to impart our experience to the new recruits. Now
that I had spent twelve months on the job, I was happy to continue the tradition of dumping on all new recruits — or hazing,
as it's called.

I believe that hazing is an essential part of initiation for all jobs
that require a cohesive team to function as one unit. The military,
which has a rich tradition of some of the best hazing history has
to offer, must also create teams that function as one cohesive unit.
A military team, you understand, is one that you must be able to
trust, one in whose hands you place your life. Remember, people
shoot at those folks. Hazing has, in the past, taught recruits hu-
mility and built trust. That's not the case anymore; in the politi-
cally correct world we live in, hazing has been largely eliminated.
Now you have to respect your platoon mate's dignity. No more
tea-bagging. Military personnel mustn't shave off anyone's eyebrows as they embark on their vocational journey to learn to kill
the enemy in a kinder, gentler way.

When I first got to Station 7, I was still only twenty-two years old. I had only recently stopped shaving with tweezers and started using a grownup razor. The vets at Seven always played games with the new guys, even if the "new guy" had been on for a while. You had to be able to take a joke. Not everyone can, and the ones who couldn't didn't last long in a place as busy as Seven.

MIKE AND DOUG, TWO JOKESTERS who had been at Station 7 for years, tried to make the young guys uncomfortable with a pseudo-gay advance thing: pretending to be gay men and seeing how much they could make the kid squirm — that kind of thing. It used to work years ago, when the crews on the job were made up of men who had suffered in the trenches overseas while the Hun tried to blow them up with howitzers.

I guess I was part of the new guard, the kind of rookie who actually read books that didn't have pictures of tits in them and didn't believe a wife should be tied to the stove with a chain just long enough to reach the bedroom. (I believe a woman should make some money too so we can order takeout for dinner.) And since I had spent several years living in a part of Toronto that's now known as the gay village, the whole pretend-I'm-gay-and-make-you-squirm thing didn't have much of an effect on me. After all, I was getting cruised by real gay men every day — and they were a hell of a lot better looking than these guys.

So I withstood the guys tea-bagging me, sticking sloppy fingers in my ears, and pissing on the back of my leg while I was in the shower.

NOW, A RELATIVE VETERAN, I was one of the guys hazing recruits. Even then, we weren't allowed to haze anymore, but the attitude was that we could explain it away as a misunderstanding, and a little misunderstanding here and there never hurt anyone. The following was a perfectly planned misunderstanding.

New recruits in the hall go through a training period when

they're riding the back of the trucks and being schooled on the workings of life in the fire hall. Crimes against humanity such as changing the channel from the hockey game to *Dancing With The Stars* are dealt with swiftly and with extreme malice. Since I was the last to actually get transferred to Seven, I usually got all the shit jobs — and not just literally (unplugging toilets). Rescuing cigarette butts from urinals, for example, is a shit job, even though no fecal matter is involved. Taking recruits through orientation is classified as a shit job as well. Having a bit of fun at the recruits' expense made the task more bearable.

One of my favourite hazes was night drill, which was sprung on a couple of newcomers one day.

"Hey, did they teach you guys night drill at the academy?" I asked.

"No. They mentioned we worked night shift but they never mentioned anything specific," one of the recruits said.

Doug and I looked at each other. "You mean to tell me they assigned you guys to the busiest fire hall in the country and they didn't teach you night drill?" I said.

The rookies started to sweat and shake their heads.

"You've got to be kidding me," Doug said.

"Well, we better get started before Captain Carl finds out, because he's going to shit all over you guys," I told them.

Doug, the two recruits, and I stood before the beds upstairs in the dorm. Doug always liked a good time, and showed the two the finer points of doing hospital corners on the bed cover. Being the veteran he was, Doug then turned to me. "We just got to keep close tabs on 'em and make sure they know how to do their stuff before one of 'em gets killed."

"Or one of us," I said, unsure how an improperly made bed could kill a guy, but you can't be too safe.

"Okay, speed is the key at night," I said to the recruits. "Get into bed and arrange your clothes on the floor in order of dress: socks, pants, shirt. We'll time you. Cool?"

They nodded.

"Good. Hurry up then."

The recruits stripped down to their T-shirts and underwear and carefully laid out their clothes just as we had suggested, then tucked themselves into bed. Doug and I went downstairs to get a coffee and let the recruits sweat it out for a couple of minutes.

Back upstairs in the dorm, Doug and I inspected the clothing layout. The recruits waited, still tucked tightly in their beds.

"Good. Nice spacing on the pants," Doug said to the recruits. "We'll bang the gong and time you to see how long it takes to get to the trucks."

Again, they nodded.

Doug and I turned to leave. "I can't believe they didn't teach them night drill," I said to him.

"Yeah, I know."

Doug and I passed the perpetually pissed-off Captain Carl on the staircase. Doug turned to him.

"Hey, Cap, you'd better check on your recruits. They're sacked out upstairs."

Captain Carl burst into the dorm to find the new recruits tucked snugly into bed in the middle of the day. His internal temperature spiked and he went supernova. "WHAT THE HELL ARE YOU DOING?!"

16

A New Life

ON THE ADVICE OF MY fellow firefighters, Linda and I saved as much money as we could for a down payment on a house. Linda was working as a nurse making decent money in a hospital downtown and we rented a one-bedroom apartment within walking distance. We skimped and lived off her salary while banking my entire firefighter salary for a year. In the summer of 1987, we bought our first home. It was the perfect starter house: a tiny two-bedroom semi-detached in a blue-collar neighbourhood.

I embraced my new role as husband and homeowner, patching up leaks in porous basement walls and replacing light fixtures while Linda planted flowers and decorated. We loved our little neighbourhood. Children played hopscotch and road hockey in the street in front of our home. A pair of sisters from a couple of doors over used to come and swing on our front gate. As a kid I dreamed of having the classic nuclear family complete with white picket fence and station wagon.

On a cold January night, we were awakened by a man banging on our door screaming "Fire!" I jumped from bed and peeked through the blinds. Flames next door to us were rolling out over the street. I couldn't tell where the fire was coming from, but worried it was coming from our house or the house attached to ours. I told Linda we had to get out. She was pregnant with our first child and slipped down the last couple of stairs as we rushed out. Fortunately, she wasn't hurt. We ran out the front door as the first fire trucks arrived and saw that the fire was not in the house attached to ours but one over from us.

The upper floor of the detached home was fully ablaze. Linda stood on our front step hugging a parka around herself and I ran to my backyard to see if the fire had spread to our house. Once in the rear of the house I saw a firefighter trying to gain access to the fire and dragging hose across our backyard. I helped him lay out the line then ran to the pump operator who was frantically trying to set out a suction line. I told him I was on the job and grabbed a hydrant for him. Once I opened the hydrant I ran back to the front of my house. I found Linda again, and we saw a firefighter come out of the burning house carrying a young girl and calling for an ambulance. It was one of the young girls who swung on our gate. A few seconds later, her older sister was carried out. As the ambulances left for the hospital and the firefighters fought to extinguish the blaze, Linda and I cried.

Flames pushing out the windows turned into smoke and steam as the firefighters pushed deeper inside. When I saw a couple of tarps being brought into the house after the fire was knocked down, I knew the two sisters had lost their parents. They would be carried out wrapped in tarps to shield their burned bodies from curious eyes.

The next morning, Linda and I went to the Hospital for Sick Children and brought a teddy bear and balloon for the sisters. We arrived at the nurses' station to drop off the gift and asked about the condition of the girls. Both had perished.

The summer after that fatal fire, we were blessed with our son. As the doctor checked him over, I saw him for the first time and my whole way of looking at life changed forever. No longer was

I going to be the reckless firefighter diving into a dangerous situation with little regard for my own safety. Now I had a little boy depending on me.

17

Back in Battle

GANG FIGHTS BETWEEN RIVAL CREWS are common in any big city, particularly in low-income neighbourhoods. Regent Park was a hot spot for tensions, many of which involved street gangs fighting for drug turf, but also grudges between cultures that went back generations (and in some cases centuries). Their parents must have been so proud.

You could lie in your bed in the dorm at Station 7 and count the gunshots. One night a bullet came through the window of one of the truck bays. *This is not good*, I thought. The upper management called an emergency meeting. This was just after the Los Angeles riots, which occurred following the acquittal of fourteen police officers in the beating of Rodney King. An L.A. firefighter was shot while driving a fire truck to put out one of the hundreds of fires set that night; the bullet passed through the driver's door and paralyzed him.

The chiefs and city planners of Toronto talked about bullet-proof glass and armour for the fire trucks, but such ideas were cost-prohibitive. Times were always tough, it seemed. To address the problem of stray bullets being fired at the fire hall — and to prevent me and my fellow firefighters from being murdered — the planners and upper management arrived at a solution. They put forward two recommendations: First, we were to wear our helmets to medical calls so as not to be confused with the police. Second, each truck was to be given an extra crew radio. At the time, only the captain and the senior firefighter carried a portable radio.

At Station 7 in Regent Park I was getting a gut full of tough fire-fighting and rough situations. Nothing seemed to faze me anymore. The unusual had become prosaic, mundane. I guess it's like a drug: at first it takes only a little bit to get torqued, but the more you do it, the more you need to get off.

One beautiful summer morning I drove my beat-up Volvo to work past all the newer cars in the public housing parking lots before pulling up to the hall. Three police cruisers were cluttering our parking lot. Great. Where was I going to park?

Inside, the floor was slippery with blood and the place was filled with screaming and yelling. *They really should clean up the floor*, I thought. In the floor-watch room I found several police officers and my workout buddy Barry, who was holding a pressure bandage to a man's neck. The man's throat had been slashed. Blood was squirting out onto his shirt and splashing to the floor.

"Hey, Barry, how's it going?" I asked. "Coffee on yet?"

"Naw, didn't get a chance."

As I got down to the important business of making coffee, the coppers were trying to get information out of the victim, such as "Who slit your throat?" for starters. He told them "some black guy" did it.

"Anything more specific than just 'a black guy'? What did he look like?"

"I don't know. Just a black guy." Hmmm.

"What was the man wearing?"

"I don't know. Black-guy stuff." It's neat to watch six or eight pairs of eyeballs all roll at the same time, like some really cool special effect.

As the cops and firefighters were trying to stop their feet from sliding in all the blood, a woman barged in. "I want that son of a bitch charged!" she demanded.

"Hey, baby," gurgled the guy through his slit throat.

"Okay, who the hell are you?" the police asked.

"I'm his wife, and I want that piece of shit charged."

"So do you know who did this to him?"

"Yeah, I did," she said.

Okay, this should be interesting, I told myself.

Turns out the guy was getting a blowjob from a neighbourhood hooker when his wife caught him. She slit his throat with a kitchen knife.

As I mopped up the blood on the floor, I wondered how the police were ever going to sort out that little situation.

18

A Fortunate Rescue

IN ADDITION TO STATION 7 being the busiest fire hall for medicals and false alarms, it had one of the busiest fire districts as well. On one particularly crazy night, an alarm came in for a fire on Gerrard Street. Fire was blowing out the front window of an old Victorian home that had been converted into a rooming house, and now the flames were climbing up the front of the building. The only sounds I can recall were screams and the noise of smashing glass.

Rooming houses are deathtraps. Most of the ones in Toronto were large Victorian homes that had been occupied in the 1800s by professional people and well-off families. Their spacious rooms had since been drywalled to make tiny cubicles for as many people as the slumlord could squeeze in. Typically the rooms were occupied by former (or soon-to-be) street people living at, or below, the poverty line. Every room had a tenant.

When you have lots of people plus narrow hallways in a century-old structure, there's a high risk for loss of life. It was going to take all the available crews on the scene to hold the flames at bay, plus many more to rescue the people inside. My crew was to do a search-and-rescue upstairs, above the fire, in order to extricate any tenants who were in imminent danger.

The hose team hit the flames hard enough to hold them back so we could duck in behind the fire and get in the front door. We charged straight up the stairs. The temperature inside was extreme. As the fire burned on the main floor, the heat and smoke were channelled upwards by the narrow staircase we were climbing. The act of going up a set of stairs during a fire like that is akin to stuffing yourself into a chimney.

Halfway up, my PASS alarm started whistling. This is a device with two functions: one function activates a distress tone when the wearer runs out of air or stops moving for fifteen seconds — in case you get hit on the head by a beam or something and go down for the count, requiring a rescue; the other function triggers a whistling sound that notifies the wearer about intense heat conditions. Now, I'm not the sharpest tool in the woodshed, but I don't need an electronic gizmo to tell me when my hair is starting to singe and the tops of my ears are producing peculiar-looking bubbles.

My partner, Mark, and I bailed from the heat. We had just emerged from the front door, our clothes still smoking, when a police officer standing next to a frantic man spoke to us. The guy's wife was trapped inside on the main floor and she suffered from Alzheimer's.

"She's all I have! Please, God, save her!"

We immediately masked up again and went back into the smoke. We only had about five minutes of air left in our masks — two and a half minutes to find her and two and a half minutes to make it out. No room for error.

Mark and I did a search of the front room, where the fire had been raging upon our arrival. We stumbled over a corpse that was burned beyond recognition. The fire was intense, and the body had been burning for a while; you could tell by the silhouette that the person was beyond help. When a human burns, the arms and legs curl up as the flesh cooks and dries out. I couldn't tell if it was a man or a woman.

We passed through the still very hot apartment towards what must once have been a beautiful parlour and opened a door at the rear. It was the original door to the kitchen, made of heavy oak. One side of the panelled door was charred, while the other side was covered in a century's worth of paint. Standing in the middle of the room was a confused-looking older woman in her late sixties, wringing her hands. Miraculously, there was no smoke at all in the room. All the doors were closed, which had kept the heat at bay and ultimately saved her life. We took our masks off to conserve our precious remaining air and to reassure the woman that everything would be fine.

But everything wasn't fine. The fire was still burning in the front, and now upstairs on the second floor as well, and we had no idea how structurally sound the house was. Was it going to fall down on our heads? Mark and I had to come up with a way of getting this lady out. Taking her through the heat would kill her, but the only window was above the sink and it had steel bars on it.

"Ma'am, we have to get you out of here," I said.

The back was impassable. We were in the only survivable pocket on the first floor, but we couldn't get out.

"I can't leave. My husband said to wait here for him," she said.

Just then the window smashed, blowing glass across the room. A crew outside then used heavy tools to take out the steel bars and provide an escape route for us. It turned out that the frantic man had been the one to lead our guys around the back and through the alley to our only available window.

He shouted for his wife. "Come, dear!"

She seemed very relieved. We were very relieved as well. A beautiful miracle had happened amid the tragedy.

That night after the fire we were back at the hall and sharing our war stories. I told the rest of my crew that the thermal alarm on my PASS had gone off. I checked the specs. Yep, it activates a whistling sound when it reaches 400 degrees Fahrenheit — to protect the *unit* from heat damage. The unit?! What about me? If I were sitting in a roasting pan at 400 degrees, you could baste me and make fricking gravy!

19

More Death and Depression

DEPRESSION HAD ALWAYS PLAYED A part in my life. Yes, I'm one of those people who suffer from the disease. Being a firefighter with depression isn't the greatest job to aspire to: you see death and suffering every day. Like many of my brothers and sisters, I found it very difficult to bring home stories about what I saw at work. How could I explain that I felt queasy after tucking someone's intestines back inside his pants after he'd leapt from eighteen floors up? And that I could still see the expression stamped on his face when he hit the ground?

The downside of working in a stressful environment is compounded when you can't rely on your time off from work to decompress. As a result, firefighters, cops, and EMTs have high suicide and divorce rates. I am no exception. And not everyone can put up with the sick humour we use to get through a shitty experience.

Many first responders hit the bottle. Many turn to drugs, while others turn to extramarital affairs. I submersed myself in the romantic images provided by the golden age of Hollywood. I would watch old movies over and over again. It was an escape. If I got tired of seeing the same movies, I would get lost in the tube — television. All I wanted was a wife who could cook like Mrs. Cunningham on *Happy Days* and who looked like Farrah Fawcett in *Charlie's Angels*. I felt I kept my matrimonial expectations within reach. (In retrospect female archetypes from seventies television shows didn't extend beyond the cathode ray tube of a 1970s television set.)

At the change of shifts during a day tour, we got a call for alarm bells ringing at a "frequent flyer" building, and I was driving Aerial 7. Damn. I had to be home right after work so I could have an early dinner and Linda could get to her night shift. I'd be delayed at this call for a while. This wouldn't sit well with her. Thankfully, the call was another false alarm and we cleared from it quickly. Great, I wouldn't be that late after all.

On the way back we got dispatched to another call. Linda would be pissed for sure by the time I got home. We, as young parents, were working opposite shifts so we could take care of our boy with the minimum of outside childcare costs. If I got home late, it would force her to be late for work. It was rush hour in downtown Toronto, which basically meant gridlock on every street in the core of the city. On the way to the call, as I followed the pumper through the traffic in my fifty-foot ladder truck, a dickhead in a T-Bird spotted an opening as the drivers stopped for our trucks. He darted in front of the pumper (I guess he missed the memo about the whole lights-and-siren thing).

The impact of the pumper hitting the car drove the fire truck into a utility pole. These were still the days before the crew rode in enclosed cabs, and one of the firefighters on the back was tossed out onto the street. The force of the impact spun the T-Bird around and threw it into a compact car at the curb. The collision was so powerful that the compact rolled over onto its side. The woman in the passenger seat, who had been waiting for her husband to come out of a convenience store, was now trapped in her crumpled car on the sidewalk.

I slammed on the brakes of the ladder truck and turned it so it blocked all the lanes of traffic. Live electrical wires lay across the scene from the broken utility pole. My first instinct was to run to the pumper to tend to my friend who was lying on his back in the street. Fortunately, he was strapped into his breathing apparatus, and the quick-release bracket for the mask had absorbed enough of the impact to save his life. But I was enraged. We had several people seriously injured because some dumbass had been eager to beat rush hour. And, in spite of the extent of the accident and the injuries, people were still honking their horns at us for holding up traffic.

I finally got home about an hour later than I usually did, and Linda launched into a tirade about how inconsiderate I was for making her wait. At first I was incredulous and I told her that the crew had been in a serious accident and I thought my friends had all been killed. Then I broke down crying. I needed a sympathetic ear. But I didn't get it.

20

Standing Up for Myself

I ALWAYS GOT A LOT of grief from Linda's brother, who used to be a chef but then switched to construction work. He had always acted like a dick towards me; I guess he felt I wasn't good enough for his sister. In-laws often aren't fun at the best of times — at least mine weren't. During a visit to the in-laws' place after work, I would tell Linda's brother that we'd had a pretty hot fire during the shift, and he would say things like "You don't know heat until you've worked in the kitchen of a large hotel." He had no idea I'd been in fires as hot as the oven he used to bake his muffins. Sure, his job involved working over hot stoves, but my job meant crawling inside them.

On Christmas Eve 1989, I drove up to Linda's parents' home after my day shift at Regent Park. Of course her brother started slagging me. "What did you do today, hero? Play cards and sleep?"

"No," I said. "I spent the day pulling burnt bodies out of a building." Asshole. The night before, Toronto had suffered its largest mass murder — the Rupert Hotel fire.

The fire had started at about five in the afternoon on December 23. A series of events made things a lot worse than they needed to be, and the fire turned into a perfect storm of destruction. The Rupert Hotel was a rooming house that had been built in the 1880s and, as we've seen over and over again, rapidly took a turn for the worse as the neighbourhood went downhill. It was filled with people who were down and out, most of them older men who had fallen on hard times and were barely eking out an existence. To them, *optimism* was just a word in the dictionary. The ones who managed to acquire regular employment moved out of the hotel as soon as they could.

A disgruntled tenant fed up with garbage being tossed into the hallway took it upon himself to teach the pig who was doing it a lesson. He took a lighter to the bags of garbage in the hall.

The building was just a block from Station 7, less than two minutes away, but at the time the Rupert Hotel fire started, the station was battling a blaze north of the fire hall, at another rooming house. There was a lot of smoke and people were trapped. A second alarm had been called in, bringing extra trucks from a good distance away. Since the crews on the scene were using up air cylinders for their breathing apparatus, a support vehicle, Air Supply 1, was dispatched with extra bottles.

On its emergency run, with its lights flashing and siren blaring, Air Supply reached the corner of Parliament and Queen, where the Rupert Hotel was located. The driver saw heavy smoke billowing and people hanging out the windows. Some were bailing out, landing on the bus shelter below.

The driver of Air Supply radioed in to dispatch to ask if a fire at the Rupert had been called in. Not yet. "Make it a second alarm! We have victims hanging out the windows!"

The driver ran in to help, leaving the truck's siren blaring — a very clever thing to do, because there were residents who didn't know their building was on fire, and the noise drew them to the windows to see the danger they were in. This driver's action saved many lives. But many more were not so fortunate; the fire moved fast and the smoke was lethal.

With all the closest trucks assigned to the other serious fire up the road, it would be several minutes before the next available crews would be able to save anyone. When they arrived, they had an enormous task ahead of them: multiple casualties, and victims still trapped by the fast-moving fire. When it was over, ten souls had lost their lives.

At 6:30 the next morning we arrived at work and immediately went to the still-smouldering building. The fire had required millions of gallons of water to extinguish, and the once-elegant hotel was now an ice-covered tomb. The tenant who had set the fire had got out while the going was good. He was charged with ten counts of manslaughter.

The fire had burned through the roof of the building, and a section of the roof and the third floor had collapsed into the second. We on Aerial 7 were tasked with going in alongside the police to photograph and extricate the victims. A foot or more of ice covered much of the interior. Getting those bodies out was going to be a tough job physically — but mentally even more so.

The human mind does many strange things when under stress. I don't know if it's a survival mechanism or what, but what I did that day horrifies me when I think back on it. One of the things a layperson has to understand is that any scene where people die a horrible death is our "office." It's where we work. The perspective of someone who sits behind a computer in a climate-controlled environment will be different from that of someone who regularly finds himself covered in human tissue.

My partner Mark and I accompanied the police "ident" team, taking photographs of the scene before we chopped the victims out of the ice and placed them in body bags for removal. The first victim we worked on was a man who had died face down in his bed. All his clothes had burned off and the mattress he was lying on was now just a bunch of tangled wire.

Photos were taken. We needed to place him in a body bag. Mark and I grabbed the victim to roll him over. He was stuck to what was left of the mattress. We tugged again — no go. During the fire his skin had melted and then cooled as it dripped down through the coils. We were going to have to rip his skin to get him off.

I came up with the idea of flicking him off the bed. So Mark and I each grabbed an edge of the mattress and began flapping it violently, trying to remove the guy from the wire as if we were old-time housewives shaking out linens in the morning sun. But it wasn't working, and the absurdity of the situation soon began to set in. We started giggling as we tried over and over again to get the corpse off the mattress.

Remember, context is everything. Context, plus the emotional stress the person has to deal with. A reporter once asked a machine gunner during the Vietnam War how he could shoot women and children. "Easy," he said. "You just don't aim as far in front of them when they run." Context. Emotional stress. In this sort of context, the emotional release doesn't always match the emotional input. The mind defers to a more pleasant emotion to take you away from the pain of what you're seeing.

A woman overlooking the operation from her balcony next door saw us struggling, her hand over her mouth, horrified. We finally got the man off the mattress and tried to place him inside the body bag, but he wouldn't fit. His arms and legs were curled up so we couldn't zip the bag closed. Mark and I had to break the cartilage in his arm joints to make him fit. By then my mind was getting pretty fucked up.

In the next room there was another man who had succumbed to the smoke. His body was on the floor, leaning up against the bed. The top of his head had bubbled out from the heat of the fire. The smell, like burnt pork, still hung in the air. As the police took photos, I crouched next to him, my fingers stuck up behind his head like a prank in a class photo.

We could lift up his upper body, but his legs were under the ice. We would need an axe to cut through it. After a half-hour or so I had the majority of the ice chipped away and then had to cut out the floor beneath his legs. The chunk of wood had to go in the bag as well; hardwood flooring that might once have supported a young couple on their honeymoon a century ago was now stuck to the burned legs of a corpse going to the morgue. Again we had to break his tendons and cartilage to flatten him out.

We were at it all day. Cold, wet, and emotionally numb from what I had seen and had to do, I stood silently next to a pile of bodies. I was still functioning, but all I wanted was to get the hell out of that fucking place. As I was walking up and down the second-floor hallway trying to stay warm, a police officer told me to watch out for the body. What body? She pointed, and under all the snow and ice and burnt timber, I saw the top of a head and a shoulder. I had been walking on that poor guy for hours without realizing it. My stomach, which had been so brave all day, finally let go. Most of what occurred on that day escapes my memory. I'm glad — no one needs to revisit those images.

So on that Christmas Eve, when Linda's brother snarkily asked me what I had done during the day, I let the ignorant jackass have it.

21

The Clink

IN SEPTEMBER 1990, A YEAR after Hurricane Hugo ravaged the Caribbean island of St. Croix, leaving $10 billion worth of damage in its wake, my big buddy Barry from Station 7 asked me if I wanted to go on a tropical vacation. His brother owned a resort in St. Croix that had been destroyed by the hurricane. Vacation at a resort destroyed by a hurricane? Hmmm, sounds affordable.

Labour for reconstruction in St. Croix was hard to come by, as the whole island was competing for every available hand to help with damage from the disaster. We were the solution for Barry's brother. He would fly us down and cover our food costs for the four days we were there to work. All we had to pay for was our liquor. Awesome — a free vacation! (Well, not quite free. It ended up costing me $300 for beer for the four days, in 1990 dollars, which would be something like $28,000 today.)

Ten of us went down to help put the final touches on his resort, building sidewalks and landscaping and making sure the place looked spiffy to bring back the tourists. We were to work for six hours a day and the rest of the time was ours.

"Hey, I've only got three minutes and forty seconds left of working!" somebody would yell as he counted down the seconds to beach, booze, and broads. Okay, there weren't any eligible women around, but the beach and the booze made a nice break from shovelling piles of gravel in the sweltering tropical heat.

Some of our big, burly fire guys were experts at avoiding the little work they were supposed to be doing. One dude hid under the cabins as if he were on the run from the Gestapo, while my buddy Prince liked to lean on his shovel with his hands folded, like Ken Dryden's iconic pose with his goalie stick. I too crawled under the cabins trying to escape the heat of the sun under the guise of picking up trash until a colony of red ants covered me and I had to dive into the ocean to escape to the stinging little monsters.

When we arrived, Barry's brother, Peter, kept telling us, "You are a bunch of white guys from Toronto. Don't go walking around by yourself. Don't go into a public washroom by yourself. The locals can get rough and the police are on strike. You don't want to end up in a St. Croix jail, because they're not going to be in a hurry to let you out." *Got it. You can trust us.* We nodded in unison as we looked longingly at the beach and the bar.

On our penultimate night a few of us rented a Jeep to tour the island. We were to meet up with the rest of the group for a night on the town at one of the only clubs in St. Croix that was open. It was called either the Moonraker or the Moanmaker. (The sign was damaged and missing a couple of letters.)

We did our little road trip, checking out the island. A lot of wreckage from the hurricane stood neglected and overgrown. And apparently a darker, anarchic hazard was roaming the island, ripping phones from the public phone booths and doing a bunch of other bad stuff that bad guys do. Our tour ended at an ocean-side bar where some of the guys hoped for a romantic evening drink with a cutie or two, but it turned out to be not so romantic — five guys, no ladies.

As we jumped back into our Jeep, a couple in their fifties who were loaded on drinks and also loaded down with grocery bags asked if they could get a ride back to their boat, just down the road at the pier. Walking was a tad difficult for them on the level ground, it appeared, and the darkness wasn't going to make it any easier. Sure, we were a group of clean-cut Canucks and we'd love to help.

He said his name was Crazy David. *Crazy David*. That should have been a clue. Then we got the lowdown on this guy: he was Crazy David of Crazy David's T-shirts, a cultural trendsetter of the early 1970s in Toronto, no less. With his wildly popular T-shirts such as "Makin' Bacon" (depicting pigs humping) and "Fly United" (geese in mid-flight trying to make little geese), he was singlehandedly responsible for thousands of teenagers getting tossed out of school for inappropriate clothing. (Including me. It turned out that "Happiness Is a Tight Pussy" actually meant something more than the cat drinking a martini on the front of my tee. Who knew?)

Crazy David told us he'd made eight million dollars in 1974. He was so busy, he said, that he slept in the factory next to the printing machines. But his empire came crashing down when K-Mart refused to pay for a large shipment of tees that the Disney Corporation found offensive: Mickey Mouse giving the finger. You don't mess with Disney. David told us he was on the run from a bunch of people who wanted to sue him: Disney for that Mickey Mouse and McDonald's for a picture of the famous golden arches sign proclaiming, "60 Million Burgers Stolen!"

"Don't take my picture!" he said. "The *Toronto Star* is looking for me." That wasn't going to be a problem, since none of us knew how to use a camera. He was kind of bonkers but kind of cool, in a drunken, hippy sort of way.

We reached their boat and were saying our goodbyes to Crazy David and his wife, Babs, when a guy driving a Jeep squealed past us from down the pier.

"Turn on your lights, you moron!" I yelled.

"He's stealing our car!" screamed Babs.

"Let's get him, boys!" screamed David. (There was much screaming at this point.)

Three of us and David jumped into our Jeep and squealed off after the thief, leaving Babs and a couple of our guys to keep her company. David was standing up in the back of the Jeep, holding on to the rollover bar like a machine gunner in one of Rommel's crews in North Africa during World War II.

The thief knew we were on his tail and drove like crazy, leading us into the shantytowns and through dark streets, deeper into unfriendly territory (unfriendly, that is, to white tourists). He shot down a dirt road and missed a corner at a Y intersection, smashing into one of the only lampposts to still have a functioning bulb in it. We skidded past the road but then caught sight of the Jeep and backed up to catch it. The driver had fled from the vehicle into the night.

Feeling kind of chuffed that we had successfully reclaimed Crazy David's Jeep, we pulled up behind the crumpled vehicle. Just beyond the lamppost was a freshwater station that the government had set up after the hurricane. A large car was parked there and three women and a little child were filling their water cans.

David started sprinting towards the car. Mike — a big guy and the driver of our Jeep — plus Lance White — another guy from Station 7 — and I ran after David. We thought maybe he could see where the thief had gone.

At this point the three of us fire guys were wondering what the hell was going on. I was just behind David when he screamed, "They're hiding him!"

The women got spooked when they saw a bunch of men running towards them, so they screamed and jumped into the car. David reached the car just as the women got inside. Through the half-open window he grabbed the hair of the woman in the passenger seat and started to bang her head on the glass.

"What the fuck are you doing?" I yelled at David and grabbed him, pulling him off the woman. Mike came up after me to help pin down this nutcase, and the screaming women made their getaway.

"Why'd you do that? They were hiding him!" yelled David. "You guys don't know because you're just tourists from Toronto. I know how these people are."

As the taillights of the women's car faded into the night, I was thinking we'd just leave David there to drive his junker back to the boat. Unfortunately his Jeep was damaged in the front and wouldn't start. We couldn't really strand the guy miles from anywhere, could we? With our bounty secure and Mike driving, Lance and I sat on the hood of our Jeep and pushed the battered car with our feet back to Crazy David's boat.

Back at the pier, Babs and our two guys were nowhere to be found. Maybe they'd walked to the police station to report the Jeep stolen. I guessed we'd better take the nut job there so he could report the theft and we could pick up our guys so we could go get a well-earned drink at the Moanmaker/Moonraker.

We drove through the rubble of what I'm sure had once been a beautiful tropical city, looking for the cop shop. David was still spewing his hatred of the locals and we just wanted to dump the asshole and pick up our guys.

As we pulled into the police parking lot, which was dark, we could see a large officer and the silhouettes of three women, one with her hair standing up like Don King's and pointing at us. She was incredulous, I'm sure, that the very attackers she was describing to the policeman were driving right up next to them.

The cop curled his finger at us and we, a bunch of fresh-faced, milk-drinking Canadians, collectively decided *You can't catch us, copper!* Our plan was to toss this Crazy David dude at their feet and then get the hell out of Dodge. Unfortunately, we weren't in Dodge. Before we knew it, every cousin, uncle, friend, and thug these women knew had surrounded our Jeep. They were going to kill us! Maybe the inside of the police station would be a safer place for us stupid pale-faced, milk-sucking Canadian boys.

Once inside, we were ordered to sit on a large leather couch that faced the processing desk. It conveniently backed onto a large picture window that now had a sea of angry black faces pressed up against it. We were seriously fucked, folks.

Lance decided to wait outside among the mob. You have to understand — Lance is the kind of guy who can run through a minefield chasing a balloon blowing in the wind, not get a scratch, and find a twenty-dollar bill in the process. He'd be fine, I was sure. Back inside, Mike and I were sitting on either side of Crazy David. The cop came in and told us we were going to be charged with assault and attempted rape. *What?*

I was not happy. I had a baby about to be born back in Toronto and I was being thrown in some foreign clink for something I hadn't done. Visions of me in the movie *Papillon* danced through my head — starving, my teeth falling out of my head because of lack of nourishment, spending years devising ways to escape the island fortress.

Crazy David, in an uncharacteristically lucid moment, turned to us and said, "I've been in jail before. They want me. They don't care about you guys. Just make a run for it. They don't have enough cops on duty to chase you." (Thinking about it now as I write this, all they needed was one cop waiting at the airport two miles down the road to nab us as we tried to get on a plane.)

Mike and I looked at each other. Run for it? Yeah. Okay, on the count of three. One … two … *bonk, bonk!* A large man, possibly the husband of the woman, was hitting the window. Unbelievably, there were even more men gathered out there now. While it was true there weren't enough police on duty to stop us from running out of the station, there were also not enough cops to stop the mob outside from slicing us to pieces. Um, we'd stay.

We were led into an interrogation room. I sat for what seemed like hours wondering whom to call to get us out of this mess. I had never had a lawyer and didn't know any.

Finally the officer came back in and told us the affair has been straightened out. The woman's family was going to sue Crazy David in civil court because the cops were on strike and wouldn't pursue the charges. Our charges had been dropped and we were free to leave. Holy of holies!

I took about two steps before I remembered the seething mob waiting for us just outside the door. Oops, still seriously fucked. The cop pushed us out the door and locked it behind us as we came face to face with the horde surrounding our vehicle. Could we just sort of inch our way forward and sneak away in the Jeep right in front of their eyes? I didn't think so. Mike and I clenched our fists in preparation for the inevitable attack. Sweat was dripping into my eyes and I quickly wiped it away so it wouldn't impair my vision.

The men surrounded us. One of them, the big one who had banged on the window when we were waiting to be booked, moved towards me. I looked around. Should I strike the first blow? I wasn't going to go down like a coward without taking a couple of those pricks with me.

The man stepped in front of me, reached for me ... and extended his hand to shake mine. "Thank you for pulling that asshole off my wife," he said. Holy balls in hell, the man was not going to kill me after all.

There was more shaking of hands from the rest of the men. I saw Lance standing in the middle of them with a stupid little grin on his face. I grinned back, silently thanking him, knowing that the guy who could walk through a minefield unscathed had defused the entire situation by explaining what had really happened at the water station.

My hands continued to shake on their own for a couple of hours. There was much drinking at the Moonraker/Moanmaker.

22

A Family Man

DESPITE MY DEPRESSION, LIFE WAS going well. I loved the guys and where I was working. The job was tough, and crazy stuff happened every day, but I felt invincible. And my family life was good; I was now twenty-seven years old, owned two houses and a new car, travelled overseas, and had a young son and another kid on the way. When the older guys at the station would spew about divorce and bankruptcy and living in your parents' basement after your wife threw you out of the house, I didn't think it would apply to me.

Shortly after returning from my adventure in the Caribbean, Linda and I were blessed with another healthy son, Michael.

I loved being a dad. In the mornings when Linda went to work I would get the boys ready for the day. After breakfast I put the two in the stroller and rolled them down to the park. We had a great time, and it afforded me the opportunity to be a kid again, playing with model rockets and hanging out at the playground.

As the sons of a firefighter, Justin and Michael knew that for every birthday they were guaranteed to get at least a fire truck or two for a present by a grandparent or other family member. At

school the children of a firefighter could count on their parent
being called into their classroom to explain fire safety and show
what a firefighter wears and how he or she does the job. Whenever
I brought in my fire gear and addressed the class of five- and six-
year-olds I could see the pride in my boys' eyes. They would become
the envy of many of their classmates. *Your dad's a firefighter? That's
so cool!* I felt proud that I could provide that for my boys.

I would pick them up from school and bring them home to
play. The house often ended up looking like a bomb had hit it,
with toys strewn everywhere. I was the biggest kid in the room
and I loved it. Then around five in the afternoon I'd be hit with
anxiety, knowing Linda would be home from work soon and
wouldn't be happy to find the house messy.

During the next year, I began to experience insomnia. Sleep was
getting difficult without the help of a sleep aid. I drank NyQuil
straight from the bottle trying to numb my overactive mind. In
the middle of the night I would wake up and feel compelled to
check the doors of the house to see if they were locked and that the
stove was off. I'd crawl back into bed, then I'd question whether
I in fact locked the doors, and then go back downstairs again to
check the locks and stove all over again. In my mind I knew they
were secure but I would still get up over and over again. This
nightly ritual went on for weeks. I began to bite my hand and leave
a mark as I locked the door so when I got up to bed and ques-
tioned whether I checked the doors or not I would have physical
evidence that I did it. It didn't matter. Even with the bite marks
on my hand I would go through the motions again. But, at the fire
hall, I never had the same urge.

In the following weeks my face became patchy with redness
across my cheeks. It looked like I had a wind burned face like
someone would get from skiing. I thought maybe the soap I was
using was too harsh for my skin. My temper became short from
stress and a lack of sleep. I would have outbursts, throwing
things and screaming into a pillow or cushion until my eyes were

bloodshot. For the next couple of months after an outburst I'd be fine until my anxiety peaked again or something set me off.

I went to my family doctor and broke down in his office when trying to explain what I was going through. "I don't know what's going on. I don't want to lose my family," I said. He referred me to a counsellor for a further evaluation. I met with her and explained how I felt, what I was going through, and what my home and work situation was like. We chatted for a while and she prescribed some medication to help me with my anxiety. To get a better picture of my home life and to get a more complete diagnosis of my condition, she asked that she meet with both Linda and I together. The verdict: There was an inequity in our marriage and I was suffering the consequences of feeling unworthy and insignificant.

23

A Reprieve from the Dark Side

BEFORE SITTING DOWN TO WRITE this book I was originally going to call my memoir *Burned Balls and Other Good Times*. My intention was to chronicle a series of funny anecdotes to hand out to my friends and family. But once I started writing, I discovered my life as a firefighter entailed a very dark side. Revisiting my journey into depression was a painful process but within that depressive period there was light in my life. Even though my relationship with Linda was deteriorating, my boys were a source of happiness and compassion. And life at the fire hall was going well. Our crew at Seven bonded and were truly brothers in arms. We looked out for each other. We were family. My time among my brethren gave me a reprieve from my dysfunctional marriage and kept me from sinking deeper into depression. They were the sympathetic ear that I needed to vent my hurt and frustrations. And they brought good times to my life, or if the times weren't good, they produced some good stories.

Early one Sunday morning we were working away at the traditional fire hall breakfast of eggs, brown stuff (usually burnt potatoes), toast, and what we called "red lead." Red lead was named after lead tetroxide, a red-pigmented anticorrosive added to primer paint used on ships during the Second World War — and it's carcinogenic. Yum! Our version was harsh stewed tomatoes that you heaped onto your breakfast.

Just like clockwork, an alarm came in for a fire, with multiple calls received at dispatch. We headed out and, sure enough, as we turned the corner onto Sherbourne Street, we could see flames rolling out of a balcony door on the third floor of a high-rise.

We humped it up the stairs and found the fire apartment. I was the entry guy, meaning I had the sledgehammer and pry tool. I broke in the door and one of the guys on the pumper crew hit the flames with water. The place went dark — visibility nil. Sometimes it makes sense to let a fire free-burn for a couple of seconds so you can look around and get your bearings. In this case I didn't have that luxury.

I tripped over and fell onto a pull-out couch that had been deployed. I checked for a sleeping victim — empty. The mattress was almost completely burned away. Almost. Its wire springs were exposed, perfect for entangling a young man's fire boots, which is exactly what happened. My foot got caught up in the burning mattress, and the flames were burning between my legs.

Today firefighters wear what's called a bunker suit. The suit is so named because it encapsulates your body and protects it from the heat, creating a "bunker" for your body that functions much like an oven mitt. Since this was a time before we got bunker suits, we still wore high rubber boots and a long canvas patch coat, which instead of acting like an oven mitt functioned more like a tea cozy, especially when draped over a burning mattress, keeping the 'nads toasty warm. The only upside to cooking your nuts is that the swelling makes them look quite impressive.

SUMMERTIME WAS GENERALLY PRETTY BUSY in Regent Park. School was out and the little jokesters were getting busy setting stuff on fire. Those darn kids! One hot summer night we were running our asses off, responding to several alarm calls in succession, when we got a call for another high-rise fire.

It was an apartment building of about twenty-four floors that had been built in the early sixties. All the buildings from that era look like they were designed by the Jetsons. This one was no exception. We went into the lobby and checked the annunciator panel, which indicates where the smoke alarm or pull station was activated. The thing was lit up like the phone lines of a radio station giving away free Justin Bieber tickets. All the lights were illuminated.

Tenants who had been evacuated to the lobby said they had seen smoke on several floors. Great. Up the stairs we trudged. Turns out those rascally kids had dowsed the inside of the elevator with gasoline and set it on fire. A laugh riot, those guys. The thing was, the elevator just kept moving, passing from floor to floor like a torch going up and down the elevator shaft. Normally when the fire alarm is pulled in a building the elevators are programmed to automatically return to the ground floor. I can only guess it didn't do this because the fire inside the elevator had corrupted or destroyed the electronics that would do this. I thought to myself, this could be bad, very bad.

The radio kept chattering. "It's on the fourth floor!" "It's on the tenth now!" "It's back down to five!" "It's at seventeen!" All this time the crews were clambering up and down the stairs, hoping to catch it when it stopped.

When it did stop, my partner, Mark Compton, and I were in the right place at the right time. Mark grabbed the hose from the standpipe cabinet and I charged it for him. Flames were licking out of the elevator into the hallway, burning the wood-panelled walls and moving up across the ceiling. In a coordinated effort, I pried open the elevator doors so Mark could stick the nozzle in and knock down some of the flames. The elevator doors wouldn't open completely, so I had to reef on the pry bar with constant pressure to keep them open for Mark. Flames were spitting out over our heads. Mark and I were both struggling, and the low-air warnings on our breathing apparatus were starting to clatter.

An apartment door next to the elevators opened and a well-dressed woman stuck out her head. We both craned our necks. What the hell was she still doing in the building?

"Excuse me," she said through the smoke. "Is there a problem? Because I've got guests and I can't leave."

How do you respond to that? I guess it's safe to assume her guests weren't a group of Mensa members.

MAE WEST, HOLLYWOOD MOVIE STAR of the 1930s, once said, "A hard man is good to find." To paraphrase a bit, I would say, "Ladies, a smart man is good to find," or "A good man is smart to find." But here was a guy who was neither smart nor a good find — our next contestant in the Regent Park Brilliance Competition, a guy I like to call Tarzan.

Tarzan, the King of the Jungle, swung from vines high above the ground to catch his prey — say, an unsuspecting jaguar — by surprise, impressing the shit out of Jane at the same time. Unlike the real Tarzan, it wasn't his girlfriend our guy was trying to impress with his high-wire antics. Instead it was his drinking buddies.

Tarzan lived in the Broadview Hotel, which, like most Victorian hotels of the era, had suffered a major slide in prestige. The hotel had hit rock bottom as yet another rooming-house type of place, but in recent years it had undergone a major facelift and a resurgence in respectability when it became home to Jilly's strip club.

As I was saying, Tarzan was drinking with his buddies — a major rooming-house pastime — and told them he had to go back to his room for something. Trying to impress said buddies, who were in the third-floor room next to his, Tarzan figured he could give his co-drunkards a scare and impress them at the same time with a display of his athleticism. He started fashioning a rope from his bedsheets, a skill no doubt learned from Wile E. Coyote in the Road Runner cartoons. (I'm pretty sure that in the novels by

Edgar Rice Burroughs, Tarzan wasn't a boozer. And, come to think of it, I don't recall the King of the Jungle ever using bedsheets to swing through the trees.)

There was Broadview Tarzan hanging out of his third-floor window with a belly full of beer and a head full of emptiness. With a mighty swing, he launched himself over to the open window of the party, yelling to startle his buddies, "This is a buuuuuust!" *Thud!*

For a couple of minutes the drinking didn't even slow down. Then, just like in a Monty Python skit, one dude slurred, "Hey, did you just see that?"

A couple of minutes went by. Then, "Hey, where did Buddy go?"

Buddy had landed. He was lying crumpled up on the air-conditioning unit of the restaurant next door.

Even in the rescue squad's Stokes basket, strapped down to a backboard, Tarzan still thought it had been a pretty cool idea.

24

Reconnecting with My Roots

HAVING LIVED IN TORONTO FOR a while and being married to a "city girl" I'd harkened back to my childhood days when I could run away into the bush to escape the stresses of life, whether it was a tough school year or fighting parents. As an adult in Toronto my outlet to escape the world of a dysfunctional marriage was limited to driving my beat-up Volvo to the Beaches section of the city and sitting in a parking lot, listening to the radio, until I had defused enough to return home to my caustic marital environment.

Often, when the kids were asleep and I didn't want to face Linda, I'd call Geraldton and talk with my brother-in-law, John Marino, who by now had become the Chief of the Geraldton Volunteer Fire Department, and relay some of the craziness I encountered as a firefighter in a large city. He got a kick out of some of the stories. There may be weirdness or bizarre situations that we dealt with in the rough sections of Toronto, but the thing is, the fires I fought as a professional firefighter in the city, in many respects, are the same dangers and difficulties faced by volunteer firefighters — men and women who do it out of duty instead of a paycheque. Hats off to volunteer firefighters everywhere.

I phoned my sisters Brenda and Chereyl regularly to catch up on local gossip back in Geraldton and to let them know I was making out okay. Mom and Dad were never much to talk. Conversations with them were kept until we met face to face whenever I drove back to my hometown to visit and recharge my small-town-boy batteries. As that small-town boy, my two older sisters wouldn't give me the time of day, but as an adult I couldn't ask for better sisters.

Chereyl being the older sister was always the level-headed pragmatist who continued, into my adulthood, to take care of me, feeding and giving me a place to stay when I went back home to visit: an extension of the babysitting role she inherited as the oldest sibling. Brenda and I got on like a house on fire. We both had a devil-may-care attitude that served us well in our lives. To heck with cleaning out the dust bunnies under the bed: people were more important than things. Make a positive impact in someone's life. The things you do in life are more important than the things you have.

As a teenaged boy I remember Brenda, at seventeen years old, telling Mom that she was moving out. "Where to?" said Mom.

"You know. With Donny."

Mom cried, mortified of what the neighbours would think of her "loose daughter."

Brenda, pregnant, moved in with her boyfriend Donny Abraham and they were married shortly thereafter. Dad went to the wedding, but Mom boycotted. There's a wonderful picture of my smiling dad standing next to the happy bride, a bump in her tummy showing. Brenda and Donny ended up living in a tiny home with their young daughter. Work was hard to come by for the young family, but they made ends meet. Donny and John, Chereyl's husband, became the older brothers I never had, teaching me how to shave and giving me tips on how to be a responsible man. Like my father, Donny was the salt of the earth and is a guy that would give you the shirt off his back and John was always telling me to smarten up and stop swearing so much.

As a teenager I had lent Brenda and Donny my stereo for a week so they could test-drive a sound system they wanted for their little home. Having finished trying it out, they were dropping it off at my house when we turned to see a cloud of smoke in the distance coming from the mine town site, which is where Brenda and Donny lived. Their home had burned to the ground, destroying the meagre furnishings, baby toys, and photos their new family had managed to acquire. We were devastated, but Brenda, being the eternal optimist, just said, "It's only stuff." Brenda wasn't a glass-half-full kind of person; she was a whatever's-in-the-glass-is-enough kind. She was the kind of person I wished I were.

I loved Toronto and the excitement of the big city, but I often missed my roots. Fortunately there was always just enough of a taste of Geraldton at just the right time to keep my foot back in Northwestern Ontario.

One time while driving the aerial downtown after clearing a call on Yonge Street, Toronto's main drag, I heard, "Hey, you're from Gerbaltown!" It was the cousin of a neighbour I used to play with as a kid, visiting in Toronto.

The first time I went to the Marine Fire Station to work on the fire boat, I met the marine engineer from the night shift. He looked at me for a second then asked if I was from Northern Ontario. I told him I was. Then it struck me: "You're the guy with the green pickup that used to come into Marino Hardware!" Sure enough, the marine engineer on the fireboat in Toronto harbour is from Geraldton, Ontario. Such a small world.

On another occasion, our crew was sitting in the floor-watch room at the start of a night shift when I recognized a man walking by the window. "That's Mr. Jacobson, my high school vice principal!" I said. What are the chances? He just happened to stop at my fire hall, while I was on duty, looking for directions. Jakey, as we affectionately called him in school, was just as surprised to see me. The crew in the hall jumped on the opportunity to make fun of me. "Was Bryan the class valedictorian?" asked one guy.

"Are you kidding?" said my vice principal. "I had to beg the teachers for enough marks to pass him and get him out of town to Toronto."

25

Elvis Is in the Building

SOMETIMES OUR STATION 7 REPUTATION preceded us. Our reputation across the city was that we were a bunch of mind-numbed cowboys who kicked ass at fires, which was bang on the money. About once or twice a month, we at Seven would get relievers from across the city. Relievers are crews who cover for those who are off sick or on vacation. That was how we met the King. Sit down, fry yourself a peanut butter and banana sandwich, and let's talk. Thank you. Thank you very much.

He came from a sleepy fire hall in the west end. He was young, full of piss and vinegar, and he had sideburns that slashed across his jawbone like lightning bolts. Cocky and intimidating. This guy kept going on about the stories he had heard about the station and how he wasn't impressed.

Elvis kept looking at his watch, expecting an alarm to come through. After all, this was the busiest fire hall in the country. It was a Sunday morning, so we had our traditional breakfast of eggs and burnt stuff, but still nothing was happening. No calls. The day dragged on. We were full of shit, according to Mutton Chop Boy; we had made up the stories about how crazy Regent Park was to make us feel like we were big men. This guy was going to blow the top off of the myth. Be careful what you wish for, bonehead.

"Just wait, kid. The shit will hit the fan soon enough," we told Elvis.

We waited all day, readying the fan for impending turds, but nothing happened. Quiet. Dead. Boring as hell. So my buddy Barry, who worked on the aerial with me, a big power-lifter kind of guy who could sell insect repellent to a hunk of cheese (I don't know what it means either; it just sort of rolled off the end of my fingers), decided this a-hole needed a good story to take back to his own fire hall.

Elvis was in the weight room working out. The weight room at Seven was a spare room full of workout equipment rescued from garages and basements. The walls were mirrored, like in the gyms from Arnold Schwarzenegger's *Pumping Iron* days, before men did yoga and Pilates.

Both Barry and I had been serious "ironworkers" for years, and we had the muscle to prove it. We were going to show this wimp how to train the way the boys at Seven trained. He was sitting there doing his dainty little curls with his tiny little weights when Barry and I walked in for our workout session. We both wore our lifting shoes — hard-soled boots that provided support for the crushing poundage we were accustomed to lifting — plus serious leather gloves with a reinforced grip, wrist straps to assist with maximum dead lifts, and heavy-duty weight belts strong enough to lift a tractor ... and nothing else. Balls naked.

I stood next to Elvis, my singed testicles just inches from his face. The cocky expression (no pun intended) had left his face, replaced by a blank stare. Our mission complete, Barry and I clothed ourselves and went downstairs to wait for the night-shift crews. Elvis could now crawl back under his rhinestone blankie and tell his crew at home that, yes, we at Seven were all screwed.

At around four in the afternoon our relief started to come in, and Elvis was sitting on the couch by himself in the TV room. Donny, a boy who hung around the hall for years, and Bobby Pimples both came by to visit. Bobby Pimples (not his real name, but the handle stuck to him for obvious reasons) was another benevolent boy of fifteen or so who dreamt of being a firefighter. There was a bit of a turf war between Donny and Bobby at Seven, both of them scrambling to be our go-to for trips to the corner store.

Donny, to prove his toughness to Bobby (and show off his affection for professional wrestling), asked the guys to give him "slammies," which basically meant holding him in a bear hug and then tossing him against a wall. Seriously — the kid loved this shit. He'd knock pictures off the wall and occasionally dent the plaster on impact. But Donny was getting to be a big kid, and he would tire us out with this stuff. Bobby, on the other hand, liked to show off his creative side by either singing into the PA system — which we appreciated, because the screeching sound chased the mice out of the hall — or breakdancing to the music videos on TV.

Elvis was privy to the "Rumble in Regent Park" between Donny and Bobby Pimples. The TV was at maximum volume as Bobby rocked out for us, spinning and flopping down on the floor in makeshift splits (damaging some internal organs in the process, I'm sure) while Donny had the guys take turns giving him slammies against the wall. The place was spinning like a barroom brawl on Saint Paddy's Day when a drunk man stumbled out of the washroom. Apparently he had been sleeping there most of the afternoon. The drunk pulled a harmonica out of his pocket and started playing a jig, at the same time dancing across the floor next to the spinning Bobby Pimples and Donny the Slammer.

By this time Elvis was curled up on the couch in a fetal position. We never saw him (or the drunk) again. Later we got a letter from the district chief asking what we had done to the guy — he had refused to work at Seven ever again. Elvis had left the building.

AFTER THAT BRIEF RESPITE, OUR call volume returned to normal; back we went to the craziness. One night we answered a medical call for a woman who had attempted suicide by slashing her wrists. The call was to one of the public housing units we visited frequently.

A shirtless man opened the apartment door and told us to screw off, that he didn't want us around. We could see a woman in distress slumped on the couch. I told him we weren't going to bother him and just wanted to help the woman. Thinking that things could get pretty hairy, my captain stepped back and radioed for the police to respond to the call.

This guy was going to be a problem. He opened the door and stepped back into the middle of the blood-splattered room. The place was covered in dozens of beer bottles. I was thinking they'd been drinking since the previous night, because it was eight o'clock on Sunday morning and the guy was still loaded.

The woman, covered in blood, was slumped on the couch. Also on the couch was another man, sawing logs. I guessed that the guy standing up was the woman's boyfriend. He was quite agitated because he didn't want the police to come around. I told him we were there just to help his girlfriend, who at that point was moaning quite a bit.

We tended to the woman and tried to stop the bleeding. The man was winding himself up and kept saying he didn't want any cops around. I told him to relax. He took exception to this comment from a mere kid, because he was thirty years old and had cancer. (I guess it was my fault for causing his cancer.)

He started pushing me a bit because I was tiny next to my partner, a mountain of a man named Steve Black. I didn't have time to get into a fight with the guy; there was a woman who had serious cuts on her wrists. At that point the paramedic crew arrived in the hallway. Buddy didn't want them to come in, and he kicked the coffee table, sending beer bottles flying. He started knocking things over and screaming at us as if we — we being "the man" — had ruined his life and given him cancer.

During all this screaming, breaking of beer bottles, and the hemorrhaging woman squirting blood all over herself, the guy who was passed out on the couch got up, stepped over the prone woman, and staggered into the bathroom, leaving the door open so we could hear him take a whiz. After finishing, he staggered back sloshing through the blood on the floor, stepped over the woman again, and plopped back down on the couch to resume his slumber.

26

Both Ratushniak Boys
Become Firefighters

A FEW YEARS AFTER I got on the fire department my brother Adrian followed in my footsteps moving to Toronto to try to become a firefighter. I introduced him to a friend of mine from the fire hall who gave Adrian work helping him renovate homes while Linda connected him with a fire prevention officer she met who advised on the application process. Toronto Fire hired Adrian in 1989.

Dad couldn't make the journey to Southern Ontario for Adrian's recruit graduation but Mom did. She wanted to see both of her firefighter boys together. But, at the time of Adrian's graduation ceremony I was working a night shift. Vacations and lieu days (days off in lieu of a holiday) had to be booked in advance. I had no way of knowing if his graduation would fall on a day when I was on duty or not. Fortunately, our truck was one of a couple selected to perform a live fire demonstration for the family and friends of the graduating class. Mom would get to see us both after all. My captain that night, a grumpy guy counting down the days to his retirement, gave us a pep talk as we set up the hose lines on the academy fire ground: "Don't fuck this up."

Linda had come to see Adrian's graduation and brought Justin, who was about a year old, in a stroller to show him his daddy in "action" on the fire ground. After the recruits received their hats and medals in the auditorium, the audience was led outside to watch a few demonstrations on the fire ground.

Our crew had pre-connected the truck to a hydrant and laid out handlines for the emergency scene our crew was simulating: a car explosion with a rescue of the occupant — a stuffed dog — and subsequent extinguishment of the fire. We were briefed ahead of time concerning the car fire. A special-effects technician had set explosive charges in the car under the hood and in the trunk for "great dramatic effect." To protect the audience and firefighters the trunk and hood were attached with chains so as not to fly off and injure someone as a result of the detonation. The technician told us to stay back a bit until the explosives went off: the force of the blast could send pieces of metal, the hood and trunk, whipping off to either side of the car, possibly injuring or killing someone standing too close. In the back of my mind I remembered the damage inflicted by a little blasting cap when I was ten years old, and I was a bit trepidatious, to say the least.

The crowd filed out from the auditorium and gathered behind a fire line. An emcee set up the situation: Sparky the Dog was trapped inside a burning car. I could see Mom, Linda, and Justin watching. "Don't fuck it up," reiterated my captain.

A deafening blast blew the hood off the car: the safety chain performing perfectly. Our crew sprung into action to extinguish the flames blowing out of the engine compartment while I approached the burning car from the side to extricate the stuffed dog. Weren't there supposed to be two blasts? *Don't fuck it up.*

While my crew hit the flames with the hose stream, I ducked in behind the fire to open the door and pull out Sparky the Dog. I tucked him under my arm taking him away from the burning car and sat him down in front of the crowd. I waved to the boys and girls watching.

"And Sparky the Dog is safe and sound thanks to the brave firefighters. Let's give them a round of applause," said the emcee.

As the crowd began to disperse I came up to Justin and said hi. He gave me a smile like he always did. I asked Linda, "What'd you think?"

"Did it have to be so loud?" I told her there was supposed to be a second blast but it didn't detonate. She laid into me, about how stupid I was, for putting myself in danger like that. But, isn't that the situation firefighters face every day? In real life there would be no way I could have known there'd be two blasts or one blast or an explosion at all as we pulled up to an emergency situation. I was proud to show her I had a pretty exciting job, but all I got, once again, was a put-down.

With the ceremony winding down, Mom told my brother and me she was proud of her two firefighter boys. As I helped my crew pick up after the demonstration, I looked over to her a few times. She had a smile on her face every time. Mom took a photo of Adrian in his dress uniform with me next to him in my fire gear that ended up on the front page of the *Geraldton Times Star*. The headline said, essentially, "LOCAL BROTHERS GET JOBS." Later, after the festivities, Mom and Adrian went out for dinner and I went back to working a busy night shift in Regent Park. I stewed a while over the jab I'd received from Linda. She didn't get it. Every fire or explosion I respond to is dangerous. That's the point of being a firefighter: To deal with dangerous situations. If we don't do it, who will?

27

Back into the Fray

A FIRE CAN START AT any time of the day, but it felt to me that statistically more blazes started when firefighters were on the toilet, in the shower, or sitting down to eat. Civilians are vulnerable to the same statistical realities. This particular blaze was started by us firefighters sitting down for dinner.

The alarm came in for a fire in an apartment located over street-level stores. It was on Queen Street East in a block of buildings built in the late 1880s. We arrived to find black smoke puffing out of a window on the third floor.

Gary Christianson was the guy we called "Grasshopper," after David Carradine's character in the seventies TV show *Kung Fu*, because he knew karate and could kick your ass. He and I ran up the stairs to do an immediate search while the hose team set up the fire-attack line. This building was very old, so it didn't have built-in standpipes in the hallway. Hose would have to be dragged from street level up the stairs to the apartment. It would take a minute or more — no time to waste.

At the top of the stairs, on the third floor, we found a man in his underwear, bleeding from the head. He had been in the shower.

(Statistically this was a double whammy of probability: firefighters eating plus a civilian in the shower. Wow, sort of like seeing
Halley's Comet during an eclipse!) Realizing that his apartment
was on fire, the man had tried to rush out through the thick smoke,
run into a doorframe, and knocked himself senseless. The guy's
eyes were still rolling around in his head; he couldn't string together
a sentence to tell us if anyone else was inside.

We crawled into the smoke. A person wouldn't be able to
survive long in that stuff. We were totally blinded by the smoke.
Gary and I got separated because I was caught behind some sort
of furniture I couldn't get around.

Fire was now building up in the corner and starting to climb
up the wall and across the ceiling. We could see the outlines of the
windows through the smoke. There was relatively little heat and I
could see that the top of one of the windows was already broken,
which was why smoke had been showing when we arrived. We
needed to get rid of some of it if we were going to be able to find
anyone in the darkness.

I smashed one of the tall, narrow windows with a tool to clear
the smoke. Almost immediately, visibility improved. What I hadn't
noticed in the darkness was how high the room was. This was
a century-old apartment with twelve-foot ceilings; no wonder I
couldn't feel the heat down at floor level. At the ceiling the temperature was hot enough to break the top of the window: upwards
of 1,000 degrees Fahrenheit.

It was only then that I realized my error. Instead of cooling off
the room and clearing the smoke, which would normally have
been the case under those conditions, I hadn't accounted for the
height of the room concentrating all that heat. *Whumph!* The
fire, fed by the air I'd just let into the room, was now in a rollover
situation. This phenomenon is created when the smoke at the top
of a room has sufficient heat and — courtesy of my window-
smashing — enough oxygen to actually *set the smoke on fire*.

A huge carpet of fire began rolling across the ceiling. Gary and

I looked at each other, his eyes as big as saucers. We both realized we were in deep shit. We had to bail out. Now. There was no time to wait for ladders to be set up for our escape. I looked outside to see where I could jump. We were on the third floor, so we'd survive, but electrical wires were blocking our path to the ground. We'd get hung up on the power lines and get electrocuted. We were stuck.

By then the other windows had blown out and the carpet of fire was racing across the room towards us. We couldn't get back to the door, so we did the only thing possible: we straddled the windowsill, with one leg outside and one leg inside, and turtled. Flames rolled over our backs, burning our skin under our coats.

Ironically, the tall windows that had originally misled me as to the heat situation ultimately saved our lives. The fire had enough room to roll out over our heads without enveloping the entire opening we were sheltered in, saving us from being cooked like a couple of boot-wearing pork roasts.

It was over as quickly as it had started. After the fire had got its initial gulp of air, it escalated and blew out the windows, ultimately cooling the room enough for the flames to abate. The Big Guy had been looking out for us. Thank God (literally).

PEOPLE PHONE 911 FOR ALL kinds of stuff: car accidents, fires, public service calls. Like when the apartment upstairs floods because the guy started filling his tub for a bath and then decided to go grocery shopping, and it overflows and the water leaks through your ceiling. Sometimes they call because they smell gas or some other strange odour is permeating the area.

I love cellphone Samaritans. "Oh, yeah, 911? I passed a street a while ago and I thought I smelled gas or something. ... No, I can't stop, I've got a meeting. ... No, don't know exactly where, but back there a few blocks." Thanks, bud, for your concern.

It was another busy day at work when we got a call for a strong smell coming from a unit on the fifteenth floor of an apartment building. We got suited up in breathing apparatus and the whole deal and walked up to the front of the building. You could smell it from street level.

"I'm going to need some coffee," the captain said to me. I agreed and we went back to the truck.

The recruit we were dragging along on the truck gave us a *What the — ?* kind of look. "Hey, Cap, shouldn't we investigate? You can smell it here at street level," he said.

"There's no rush," the captain told the kid.

On the fifteenth floor the elevator door opened and the crew immediately started to gag. We put on our breathing apparatus. We found the apartment. A note was taped to the door asking the tenant to do something about the terrible smell.

I bent down to look through the mail slot, turned to my captain, and nodded. It was kind of funny to see the confusion manifested on the recruit's face. *Watch and learn, kid.*

I took a sledgehammer and knocked in the door. It swung open, pushing against a large pile of flyers and mail. There on the floor lay the decomposing body of a woman.

The captain said, "Okay, let's have that coffee." I took a pot out of the cupboard and placed it on top of the stove. By now the recruit was wondering, *What the hell is happening here?*

I turned the burner on high and produced a packet of coffee from inside my coat, ripped it open, and poured the contents into the pot. It immediately started to smoke. I took off the facepiece of my breathing apparatus. The smell was gone.

The rest of the crew took off their masks. The captain keyed the mike on his portable radio: "Control, we have a person who expired some time ago. Request police and ambulance."

The recruit stared at the lonely soul. She died alone. Her body had been decomposing for so long that it was now desiccated, shrunk to only a few inches high — prune-ified. It was lying in a pool of congealed blood.

There was nothing we could do for this person, so we backed out of the apartment and closed the door, leaving things for the police to take over. We stood in the hallway and explained to the arriving officer what we'd found. He was a vet. He'd known as soon as he got off the elevator what had happened.

The tenant from the next apartment approached. "Are you here about the smell?"

We told her yes.

"Good, because whatever she spilled in there has been leaking into my apartment. I've been cleaning it up for days." I was beginning to feel the mental burden of the sheer volume of dead people I had to deal with.

28

You Can Only Go Down So Far

I ALWAYS WANTED TO BE famous whether I was a rock star or a hockey player or an actor. Although I had taken an acting in television class, which was basically a scam that preyed on rubes like me coming to the big city hoping to become a star, I had yet to appear on television with the exception of catching a glimpse of myself at a fire, once or twice, in a televised newscast.

I trained in a gym close to my apartment six days a week on my journey to become a competitive bodybuilder. A man who worked out there had occasionally asked me for training tips. His name was Craig Alexander and he was one of the top casting directors for film and television in Toronto. We became friends and he told me he was running out of "beer guys" to send to auditions. He asked if I'd like to be in commercials. Of course I would! *Everyone from Geraldton would see me on TV!* He said I would be a smiling prop, really, but the cash was good.

My first television spot was a Leon's Furniture commercial where I played a shirtless security officer with a Doberman guarding a bank vault. Pure art. Then I scored a beer commercial portraying an underwater sea creature because the talent needed to be a bodybuilder that had a SCUBA certificate. I fit the bill perfectly, but I almost drowned in the process.

The scene in the commercial was to illustrate a man's nightmare as he ran through a distorted Salvador Dali–esque world where an ordinary living room wall with a painting of an underwater monster comes to life. I was the underwater sea monster in the scene.

Wardrobe dressed me with a long black wig and a mesh suit covered in seaweed, transforming me into a type of creature from the Black Lagoon.

The stunt was performed underwater in a pool. A large panel was laid horizontally on the surface of the water like a floor — or a ceiling, for anyone underneath it. It was held up by scaffolding with the camera on a crane filming from overhead. From the camera's point of view the illusion was a painting hanging on a wall in a den.

Submerged under the water, two divers, who provided air via a SCUBA regulator, held me horizontally looking up to the panel, in my start position. I didn't have a nose clip like synchronised swimmers use for underwater inversion, and the air bubbles from the regulator caused me to gag. An assistant director would hit two hammers together underwater, cueing me to cast off the air regulator, hold my breath, and do my underwater dance. After I performed a take, my breath held for thirty seconds or so, a diver thrust an air regulator into my mouth, but the regulator became entangled in the wig, preventing me from getting a much-needed breath of air. I scrambled through the scaffolding to the surface coughing and gasping for air. The filming wasn't going very well.

The clients for Black Label beer showed up on the deck of the pool to watch the progress just in time to see me flail and choke under the wall as I grasped the underwater scaffolding and tried to propel myself to open water to get air. They were not impressed. "We didn't think this through," said someone on the pool deck.

I was helped out of the pool as the crew re-evaluated how to pull this stunt off. I told the producer I was choking because I needed a nose clip to prevent the water from going up my nose. A makeup artist chimed in that she could have provided wax plugs if she had known. Nobody appeared to know I was to be held upside down until we started shooting. There was much finger pointing.

Out of the corner of my eye I caught a glimpse of a discarded nose clip on the pool deck. *This should work fine.* I picked up the nose clip, pulled off the lint, clipped it on my nose, and went back to work. After three hours in the pool, my core temperature had plunged and I was shaking uncontrollably. The wardrobe man wrapped me in a towel and rubbed me down, trying to warm me up.

"We've got six feet of film left," said the director. *Christ, another take.* "Just start from the bottom of the pool and swim up to the window": the window being the "picture" on the wall that comes alive.

I jumped back into the pool. The divers held me in place, the regulator in my mouth, until the two clicks of the assistant director's cueing-hammers sent me into action. I ascended to the window, swooped back, and disappeared out of the frame. "Cut!" shouted the director.

When the commercial aired it received much acclaim for its artistic merits and gave a new lease on life to a tired beer brand. Black Label became cool. Even though I had spent over three hours in the swimming pool at Havergal College freezing and choking take after take, the shot they used for my scene was the very last one: the last six feet of film where I swam up from the bottom of the pool.

While new doors were opening for me professionally, things were not going as well for me personally. For months I had been weighing the idea of leaving my marriage. The stress of living in an unhappy home was getting the better of me. On the set of a Tim

Hortons commercial, things started crumbling for me emotionally in front of everyone. I had lost the lead in the spot; it was down to two of us who auditioned for the part and the other guy got it. I was then relegated to background performer. As the shoot went on, the guy who had taken my part kept flubbing his lines, so we had to do take after take of the same lame dialogue. My consolation for losing out on the lead role was a nonspeaking part in the production as a customer in the restaurant carrying a tray of coffee and a cupcake over to a table and sitting down.

After about thirty takes I had my part down pat. The other guy was an amateur, so, after yet another of his flubs, as any real thespian would, I got everyone's attention. Pointing to my sad cupcake, I declared, tongue firmly set in cheek, "Excuse me. My character wouldn't eat this. I'll be in my trailer if you want to talk to me." (I didn't have a trailer so I looked kind of silly walking around in circles searching for one.)

The head of wardrobe was a stylish woman a few years older than me. I had worked with her a few times before on other commercials and she took me under her wing. I told her I needed to get out of my marriage. It was killing me, but I felt I had to stay for my boys.

"Don't stay for the kids," she said. "I have two wonderful daughters who are the happiest young women you've ever met. They make me soup and take care of me when I'm sick, and they just want Mom and Dad to be happy. They don't want to see the fighting."

I remembered my parents fighting like a cat and dog and me vowing I would never put my kids through that. And here I was doing exactly the same thing. I had to leave Linda.

In the summer of 1993 Linda and I agreed that things weren't working out and we both felt a split was inevitable. Linda was to have a medical procedure done and would require a long recuperative period. I assured her that I wouldn't move out until she was well, probably not until some time in the following new year.

I told my mother I was moving out. I was going to divorce Linda. "Disgusting" was all she said. Dad just said, "Okay." Brenda and Chereyl were supportive and offered a sympathetic ear. I loved them for that. Adrian was going through his own divorce at the time, but nobody knew it. Nobody knew anything about him: where he lived, what he did, or where he went between shifts at the fire hall. At work he was known as Secret Adrian Man. He let me know that I had become an uncle to his son five months after he was born. And to illustrate that irony is not dead, he left active firefighting to become a Toronto Fire Services Information Officer.

29

The Beginning of the End

I GREW UP SUFFERING FROM depression. That's not to say that I wasn't a happy kid, but every silver lining had to have raincloud behind it.

"Hey, Kathy Popowitz has a crush on you," a buddy of mine said to me.

"Wow, I've had the hots for her since I was six," I told him. (I was seven at the time.)

"You going to ask her out?"

"Naw, she'd just dump me anyway."

I was later diagnosed with clinical depression, with a touch of ADHD thrown in to sweeten things up. Basically I was a bummed-out kid who couldn't concentrate very long on being down. I guess things sort of evened out in the end: a case of the blues with a "spinner" chaser.

One of the things I learned on my journey to combat depression was that the average person can deal with a crisis if they have enough time to decompress. Time heals all wounds, as they say. A bunch of doctors during the Second World War figured this out when they discovered that a couple of weeks away from the horrors of battle gave the soldier a longer shelf life. A minister who was a fire department chaplain told me that in his native England at the start of the war, shell-shocked soldiers were dismissed from duty with "LMF" stamped on their discharge papers — "lacks moral fibre." Jesus Christ, can you believe that?

Given that I was working at the busiest fire hall in the country, it was just a matter of time before I would be faced with the odd crisis here and there. At that point in my personal life, things were not good. My marriage had dissolved and the guilt I felt for putting my two young boys through that shit was eating at me pretty badly. Anxiety began to cripple me. All I could think about was my two beautiful boys.

THAT WEEK I WAS WORKING a fire in the west end and had been called to do a search of the second floor with the Rescue Squad crew. Inside the smoky building, I followed the crew up the stairs. Halfway up I stopped. I was choking. Not because I had run out of air — my tank was full. What was going on? I just wanted to rip off my facepiece and run.

I was having a panic attack. Inside a burning building! My chest was thumping, I was hyperventilating, and my fingers were starting to go numb. I grabbed the banister. *Get hold of yourself!* I couldn't breathe. Inside my head I was screaming. I had to get out. Now!

I don't remember how I got out, but I do remember taking off my equipment and tossing it into the street behind one of the trucks. *You're losing it, Rat. You can't let anyone see this.* All I wanted was to take off my fire gear and run. Out on the street everything looked sort of wonky, distorted, like whenever the bad guy showed up in the campy *Batman* TV show from the sixties. The image on the screen was off-kilter. Was everyone looking at me? Can they tell that I'm losing my mind? I held on to the side of the truck, anchored so I wouldn't pass out.

I made it to the end of the week. I would have a couple of days to decompress, to regroup.

Work returned far too quickly. I knew I was fragile, but being a typical macho guy in a macho job, I kept my state of mind under wraps. That day we had a fire in an apartment over a restaurant. Living up to our reputation, the guys at Seven attacked the fire with the aggression of a threatened mother bear — balls to the wall. The longer you wait, the harder it gets.

My partner Billy Handson and I each grabbed a hose line, charged up the stairs, and broke into one of the apartments on fire. It was already rolling pretty good.

We got in deep. Billy was one hell of a firefighter, and you had to be pretty good to keep up with him. Then the ceiling came down on us. We were covered in flaming ceiling tiles and insulation. We each had our own hose line, and I hit Billy with the stream from mine to put out the burning debris. The shit was hitting the fan big time. Then, as a section of the wall came down, a blast and a flash of white light knocked us on our asses. What the fuck was that? We decided to back out and re-evaluate.

At street level the blast had been heard down the block. When the interior walls came down, they'd exposed the electrical wiring behind them. I had hit the high-voltage line that supplied the commercial freezers downstairs in the restaurant. My nozzle had been set to a fog pattern to cool off Billy so he could get closer to the base of the fire. This was a good thing, because when I hit the high-voltage line, the water particles were well separated, so there wasn't a complete line of conductivity. If the nozzle had been set to a straight stream, I would have bought the farm (or at the very least a prolonged visit to the steps of the Pearly Gates) — I didn't need that. But on the plus side, I didn't have a panic attack. *Good. I'll be okay*, I thought.

That same weekend we had a subway jumper. Generally, people get hit by subway trains on purpose. In the most common scenario they jump in front of the train as it's coming into the station, with the intent of ending it all. They wait at the end of the tunnel where the train enters and, as it approaches, they jump onto the tracks in front of it. There's no time for the train to stop. It's messy; most jumpers roll up under the cars and tumble over and over. Some get twisted like a corkscrew.

In Toronto's subway system this happens about once a week. These incidents never make the papers — there are too many copy-cat idiots out there. (The majority of non-lethal subway accidents are caused by people standing too close to the edge and getting whacked on the elbow or forehead by the passing train. Stand behind the yellow line, folks.)

"Okay, Bryan," I said to myself. "We have a call for a subway jumper. It's always a yucky experience. Can you do this?" We got down to track level and found the person's shoes neatly placed on the platform — a sign that he'd planned it. A note was sticking out of the top of his knapsack.

I always feel sorry for the train operator. He or she is just trying to make it through the day. They're busting their butts like the rest of us, paying their bills and hoping to make a better life for their kids than they've had. But at that point in my life I had more in common with the jumper than I did with the driver. I was bottom-ing out pretty hard.

The train had stopped in the station and the passengers were ordered off to grab shuttle buses on the surface so they could go on their merry way. Once it was confirmed that the power was off, I slid down between the cars. As I crawled under the train in the darkness, I could see the silhouette of the jumper ahead. His head was closest to me, and I checked to see if he was alive. He was in one piece, so that was a good sign.

It was a young Asian man. He still had his glasses on; it looked like he was having a nap. I touched the back of his head. It was smashed; it felt like Scrabble tiles rubbing together in the bag that you pick the letters from. Not good — he was clearly dead. I needed to roll him over and flatten him out so we could move the train along and get him into a body bag. His arm was sticking out of his jacket. I tugged on it to roll him over and I found myself under a subway train shaking hands with ... just an arm. Another jolt to the old mental health.

The very same day, we got a police call for assistance. They had a man wanted for outstanding warrants cornered on the roof of a burger joint. He had nowhere to go, so the cops wanted us to put the aerial ladder up to the roof so the guy could climb down and be arrested. The man said he had hepatitis and was spitting at the police as they approached him.

I was spinning a bit out of control. The anxiety was starting to ramp up again. *We've got to get this asshole off the roof now or I'm going to have a meltdown right here in the street*, I thought. *Hurry up, buddy.* Then, *Christ. Fuck it!*

I climbed the ladder to the roof. The guy told me to fuck off and I told him to fuck off right back. It was a Mexican standoff, two whack jobs screaming "Fuck off" at each other. Mr. Hepatitis started spitting at me. The cops below thought I was nuts — the guy had hepatitis! He then said he was going to kill me. I told him if he did, he'd be doing me a favour. He charged at me again and launched another loogie, but he found himself facing a firefighter who had the crazed look of Old Yeller frothing at the mouth just before the kid shoots him. He stopped dead, confused.

"Get the fuck down the ladder or I'm going to go up there and throw you the fuck off the roof myself!" I said to him. He came down.

30

Firefighter Fellini or
Hitchcock Hose Jockey?

I NEEDED A DIVERSION FROM the loneliness and guilt I was feeling because of the impending divorce. That Christmas season there was one day at work when the entire crew was washing hose from a fire the night before and singing Christmas carols in our joyous, off-key way. It occurred to me that every celebrity down to the D level had made a Christmas album of the same old tunes (a couple of my favourites are by William Shatner and Ed McMahon). What's to stop a bunch of untalented firefighters from making a Christmas album just as mediocre as the ones by those guys? Marketed right, we could be the next Four Tenors, or rather the Fourteen Hose Boys. This could be our get-rich-quick scheme.

"Just make a video of fire trucks. Kids will eat that shit up," said Wayne Patterson, one of the guys washing hose. Around that time, some guy in the States had made a video of a bunch of tractors pushing dirt and stuff, and he was making a shitload of cash.

We could do that. Wayne and his buddy Steve Stephen both had great business sense, and I could be the host. I am an actor of sorts, but that means nothing in the fast-paced world of children's video production. I had acted in a lot of TV commercials, but I never got to say anything. Commercial producers didn't like my voice. They said I sounded like a movie star, but unfortunately that movie star was Demi Moore. I had even auditioned for my own voice for a Tylenol commercial in which I was the hero, and I still didn't get it. But I was my own producer now, and damn it, I was going to hire myself and use my own voice.

We saddled up the palomino and drove south on a road trip to fire stations across North America. We knew what we were doing, or at least we had an idea. We were simply going to film Rat (that's me) visiting different stations and looking at different fire trucks and trading patches and stuff with other firefighters.

We started on Boxing Day. Off we went for ten days and 5,000 kilometres — and I drove every inch of it. I had to; if I sit in the passenger seat I get carsick, and it was my beat-up Volvo anyway.

The plan was that Steve and I would videotape stuff on the way down south and hook up with Wayne in Florida. We'd pick him up from his dad's retirement condo and then drive back north, filming the whole way. This planning is called pre-production: the preparation before actual filming of a movie (or, in this case, a kid's entertainment video).

First stop: Buffalo, New York. Steve and I set off from Toronto and got lost in Hamilton, which is about an hour from Toronto. And then, because I didn't know where I was going, we missed the state of New York completely.

Take two. First stop: Detroit, Michigan. Since I still had no idea where I was going, I found out that Detroit is the only city where Canada can be seen by looking south (check it out on a map). Also, during the War of 1812 the city was captured by Canadians in the siege of Detroit before being recaptured by Uncle Sam in 1813. Anyway, Steve had been to Detroit once to see a hockey game at the Joe Louis Arena and remembered that there was a beautiful old fire station next to the stadium. So, throwing away the playbook/ route plan that charted our journey through the US from Buffalo, we set sail for the Joe Louis Arena.

Sure enough, there was indeed a beautiful fire hall next to the stadium, built, I'm guessing, in the late 1800s or around the turn of the past century. The stonework above the doors was carved into gargoyles and scenes of firefighters rescuing children. Clearly this was the headquarters of the Detroit Fire Department. The place had about seven bays for fire apparatus that had likely housed horse-drawn hose wagons and steamers when it was built.

Steve and I walked into the beautiful building. Inside we saw one sad-looking fire truck. Sheets of peeling paint hung from the ceiling. Where were the dozens of guys and hook-and-ladders and stuff that a kid from north (technically south) of the river would get a kick out of seeing? I guess I missed the memo about Detroit going through a major downturn with that whole economic crisis thing. We were told to check out another fire hall not too far away.

Coming from a culturally diverse city like Toronto, I found it quite sad that the fire halls in Detroit, according to the firefighter I talked to, were segregated into black and white. The black guys worked in the core and the white guys worked in the suburbs. The white guys in the suburbs got the new trucks and the black guys in the core got the junkers. The "trickle down" didn't trickle down to those guys. Politics was rearing its ugly head once again.

After a couple of video shoots of trucks and fire stations, we were off on another assignment: finding a bar. Being brothers, firefighters transcend all cultural and ethnic boundaries, and these guys were no exception. They were awesome. "You white boys are all right, but I wouldn't send you to any bar around here," one of them said. "Better go to Greektown." Off to Greektown we went, to drink with the other whiteys.

Next on our improvised tour, we hit Philadelphia, home of the modern fire department. It was there that the kite-flying Ben Franklin formed the first organized fire brigade (I'm guessing soon after his kite burst into flames after the lightning bolt hit it). A dispatcher from Philly Fire took us around to the different fire halls, and we even caught a little fire in a vacant lot (it was a bunch of Christmas trees). At one point we convinced a couple of kids that we were a news crew from Channel 2. They said hi on camera to their friends and parents. Is there a Channel 2 in Philly?

Back on the road we went, doing the whole guerrilla filming thing for a couple of days as we made our way south. But we were getting burned out before we had really got going on the production. The routine of the road went like this: I would drive all day, we would visit a fire station or two and videotape it, and then I would drive until one or two in the morning. I would sleep as Steve logged the footage we had shot during the day. Then the next day he slept in the car until our next city's video shoot.

WE VISITED ATLANTA, IN THE lovely state of Georgia. That city has a history of good fires, such as when General Sherman burned the shit out of the place during the Civil War. We had a meeting set up with the fire chief — awesome. Using our gas-station road map, we found out (after several wrong turns) that every street in Atlanta is called Peach–something or other, and they're all one-ways. We could even see the building we wanted to go to, but we couldn't figure out how to get there through all those damn one-way streets!

Finally we got to Atlanta City Hall. Ironically, the building stood on the site of the home of Bill Sherman, the man who had burned the shit out of the city on his "March to the Sea" in 1864. We parked the car and ran to the front door, only twenty minutes late for our meeting. Gasping for air, we told the security guard at the door that we had a meeting with the fire chief.

"He doesn't work here," said Mr. Security. What? We told him that Steve had arranged a meeting with the chief at city hall.

"His office is in City Hall East," said the guard. How stupid of us to assume that Atlanta had only one city hall.

An hour later we found Atlanta City Hall II. The chief turned out to be a super guy, and he told us his aide would drive us around for the day. We caught a fire and we talked to a lot of really great firefighters. At the end of that successful day, we took our guide out for beers.

The chief's aide told us which side of the street to walk on. "You're okay on this side," he said. "The bums will bug you over on that side." Shouldn't there have been a sign for tourists?

As we were walking along on the wrong side of the street, a street person asked me (or rather told me), "Be a man. Give me some money." We have panhandlers in Toronto, but I have to give this guy credit for having his own style. He kept following Steve and me. At one point he actually jumped on my back and wrapped his arms around my neck. I felt panicked, but being a muscular kind of guy, I instinctively flung him off me, effectively launching him against a post. Half dazed, the guy still wouldn't let up: "Be a man. Give me some money." So, being a kind Canadian, I tossed him a one dollar coin, a loonie. He picked it up. "What the hell is this?" The guy had style; yes, he did.

We picked up Wayne at his dad's place in Clearwater, Florida, to video a few places in the state before heading back up north to Canada. We were in the part of the state where the locals are featured in reality shows about swamps and gators and such when the radiator on the old Volvo gave up the ghost. We pulled into a 7-Eleven to get some water to fill up the rad and check a phone book for a rad shop nearby. I was tired and hot. I just wanted to be magically beamed back to my bed in Toronto to sleep for a week straight. Wayne wrote down the address of the rad shop and with the aid of a local map purchased at the 7-Eleven drove off to get my junker repaired.

The neighbourhood where the rad shop was located was a scene straight out of the movie *Deliverance*. Dilapidated cars and boarded-up shacks. The only thing missing was the scary looking kid playing a banjo. We spotted the rad shop by the radiators hanging like Christmas decorations from a large tree. Inside the shop the floor was flooded with radiator fluid. A young boy, with bare feet and in overalls (one brace obligatorily unhooked), came sloshing out to meet us. "Dad'll be out in a minute," said the boy. Dad came out and, just like in *Deliverance*, "sure had a purdy mouth" in need of a dentist. He looked at my Volvo and then at us three exhausted Canadians standing at his mercy. "Foreign car. That'll be thr ... four hundred dollars." Sold. Just get us the hell out of this backwater hole. After the rad was fixed we shot a few things here and there and then went on to Jacksonville for the day.

As we were driving through the city, a fire truck whizzed by. Steve popped his head through the sunroof of the Volvo and I hit the gas in pursuit of the fire truck and hopefully great video action. We caught up to the truck and stuck to its tail, ignoring red traffic lights and getting more than one astonished look from Jacksonvillians.

The fire was in a dry cleaner's just up the street from a nearby fire station. We parked our car at the fire hall and walked up to film the fire action. A group of guys started yammering at us as we walked past their house. I thought we would have another confrontation like the one on our St. Croix adventure. But, from across the street, an older woman standing on her porch yelled at our tormentors with her booming voice, "Leave those boys alone!" They left us alone all right. We waved to the woman to thank her. At the dry cleaner's we grabbed some great video of the fire which made it into *Fire Trucks and Firefighters* and Volume One of *Lots 'n' Lots of Fire Trucks*.

At four in the afternoon we finished our day's shooting. Wayne turned to me. "You have four hundred miles to drive before you can turn the car off." Fine. We'll grab some food for the road. McDonald's had a special offer going: two triple burgers for two bucks. So naturally we each ordered four, for a total of twelve slabs of greasy meat. Yum! You could hang wallpaper on our faces with the grease seeping through our pores. Steve and I had been eating burgers for a week, and felt like I was now experiencing the early symptoms of scurvy or some other malady ancient mariners suffered. The only vegetables we had eaten for seven days were mustard and ketchup.

By the time we reached Washington, DC, we were tired of bunking in fleabags. We splurged on the kind of hotel that people with jobs stayed at. By this time our bodies had gone into complete rebellion mode from all the crap we had been eating. The three of us met for dinner in the restaurant: green salad, consommé, and sparkling water.

Back in Toronto, we dumped fourteen hours of raw footage on the editor's desk and went to bed.

The road trip had given me a much-needed break from dwelling on my screwed-up life. But now that I was back in Toronto, I was confronted with reality. I had to keep that video diversion going, at least until I had got my wits about me again.

31

A New Life

I HAD MET KELLY ON December 18, 1993. Our crew from Regent Park were out for a pre-Christmas outing. I had caught a ride with a crewmate and we were on our way home after a few hours of drinking and having a great time when I saw Kelly on my way out the door. She was chatting with my buddy Lance, taken with his good looks. He introduced me to Kelly and when I saw her big blue eyes it was like lightning hit me. *You look so familiar.* We chatted for a minute or two and she asked me to dance. As my ride was ready to go, he said that he'd wait for me. I was tired and wanted to go home but reluctantly, I agreed to the dance. She grabbed my hand and led me to the dance floor. It was such a weird feeling. I felt like I had known her for twenty years. But, even though I was taken with her, I had no intension of dating as Linda and I were still living in the same house and I didn't need another complication in my life.

Kelly told me she was a corporate communications writer — whatever that was — for a large telecommunications company and I asked if I could get a deal on one of those newfangled cellular phones. She said she'd look into it and gave me her card. I told her I'd call in two or three weeks because a couple buddies and I were going to the States to shoot a fire truck video. That's why I needed the cellular phone. And hey, I could use her help as a writer for the voiceover! Of course she didn't believe me.

At home I told Linda that I had met a writer that may help with the kids' video. She had seen a psychic a few days earlier — she did this occasionally — who told her a blonde woman would enter our lives and this would lead to a financial windfall. Meeting Kelly was a good thing, it seemed.

LINDA WAS BACK TO FULL strength, recovered from the medical procedure that had stalled our separation. Our marriage hadn't improved at all during her rehabilitation. The time came when I could no longer stomach living in that caustic marriage.

Kelly and I stayed in touch and I told her that if I had the money I'd move out and get my own apartment. "You don't have to stay where you don't want to. You have choices." She said she had a place she rented with friends of hers and said I could crash on the couch until I could get a place of my own. Great. A much needed escape route.

I told Linda my plan to stay on a friend's couch for a while until I could get my own place. We agreed to keep up the same child-care duties during our separation. I told Justin, who was five at the time, that "Daddy's going to be gone at night time like when he's working on the fire truck but will come home and take care of you and Michael just like before. But now Mommy and Daddy won't fight."

"Yay!" said Justin. I gave the boys a kiss, packed a gym bag full of clothes, and walked out the door. The routine went without a hitch for a week or so: I went to work, stayed at the apartment, and came to take care of the boys when Linda was working. I was crashing at the opposite side of the city with five others. Young people just out of university, starting their careers, and then there was me: father, firefighter, fuck all. Their lives were on the upswing while mine was skidding along the bottom.

LINDA WANTED TO KEEP OUR separation secret from her parents, assuming I was just having a mid-life crisis and would come crawling back home with my tail between my legs in good time.

Then, after telling Linda that I wasn't simply trying to find myself — that our separation was permanent — she said, "You can't survive without me," harkening back to the evaluation from the family counsellor. I was starting to believe it. Maybe she was right. I wouldn't be able to make it on my own. *But I'll die here if I stay in this house.*

In the coming weeks Linda began using my depression against me. She cited the outbursts I had when I lived with her as an excuse to stop me from seeing Justin and Michael. "You're un-stable!" she said. I guess she was trying to smoke me out of the woods, trying to get me to crawl back to her. I just wanted to curl up with my little guys and cry. To let them know how much I loved them and that it wasn't their fault.

Boy, had I fallen. I used to have two houses, a new car, and a family. Now I slept on a couch in a student rental where I kept my groceries in a laundry basket in a back room, had to share one refrigerator with five others and use a hammer to bang open the rusty taps for the bathtub. Meanwhile, Linda was saying stuff to me like "The boys are so much happier now that they don't have a crazy father in the home anymore."

Depression creates a chemical imbalance in the brain, along with irrational thoughts that in your mind seem quite logical. Thoughts such as *The kids have already forgotten about me anyway* (it had been a month since I'd left). Or *They're better off with me dead. Yeah, that makes more sense. But I won't kill myself until after I finish the video — Steve and Wayne are relying on me.* Seriously, that was my thought process.

As we continued production of the kids' video, we learned as we went along. We would shoot anything and everything and then leave it to the editor to make something out of the mess of footage. Since it was a fire-truck video we were making for the little tykes, we thought, *Why not show a view of a fire truck responding to a fire from inside the cab?*

We jerry-rigged our camera to the dashboard of the pumper, using a sponge, a bungee cord, and a whack of duct tape, and aimed it out the front window. We were ready to make Hollywood magic. After all, how hard could it be? A fire call comes in, we press the Record button and then go put out a fire. We were trying to capture the view you get from police cruiser videos on those "craziest police chases" shows that play on the macho channels.

We were called to a fire in a rooming house a few blocks east of the fire hall. Smoke was blowing out of the house and across the street. *What a great visual!* A young man was waving his arms, trying to get our attention. *Wow, this looks great — a real sense of urgency. Yeah, we can see the fire. Watch out for your shadows. Yes, Mr. DeMille.*

The young man told us that some students were living up in the attic and he didn't know if everyone had got out. Shit. We rushed inside to do a search. The place was huge. There wasn't a lot of heat but there was a ton of smoke.

We got up to the top floor and found a ladder going up to a hole in the ceiling. That was the attic the guy was talking about. If anybody was up there, they were going to be in rough shape with all that heavy smoke. With our breathing apparatus on, we could barely squeeze through the opening. I was thinking, *It's a goddamned shame people have to live like this.*

Once we got inside the attic, the heat was quite intense — all the smoke and heat were trapped up there. The only windows were tiny ventilation holes at each end that were covered in plastic. The attic had been divided into little rooms by stringing ropes across the space and hanging blankets for privacy.

Visibility was basically zero and I became tangled in one of the blankets. As I was trying to free myself, I fell through the access hole. The air cylinder attached to my mask had caught one side of the opening and my ribcage was wedged against the other, stopping me from plummeting to the floor below. It felt like a bolt of lightning shot through my body and I became numb all over.

It took a couple of seconds to realize what had happened. During that brief time I had re-evaluated my whole life: I was broke, depressed because I couldn't see my kids, and it looked like I had just suffered an injury that would end my career. I thought about my boys, visualizing their happy faces and what their future would be like; I even did the imagine-your-child's-wedding-day thing.

I decided Justin and Michael would be better off with an insurance payout that could jumpstart their futures — money for their tuition or a down payment on their first home — than with a crippled and depressed old man. I had made my decision: *I quit. I give up. It's over for me. My boys will be fine. I'll just stay where I am and let my air run out. They'll find me eventually.* The line-of-duty death payout was twice as much as for a death off the job. Ironically, if I had killed myself at home because of the stress of being a firefighter, it wouldn't be deemed job-related. This was the perfect solution — suicide by work accident.

It was very calming moment. I closed my eyes and leaned my head on my shoulder as if I were having a nap. The sounds of the fire and the crews working on it became muffled as they swirled around my head. Then that prick Billy Handson ruined everything. He grabbed me by the collar and hauled me up, then lowered me down the hole to my captain. *Just leave me here*, I thought. *No, really guys. You're ruining it! I'm trying to — Aw, fuck it.*

I WAS SENT TO HOSPITAL strapped to a backboard. What else could go wrong with my life? The ambulance crew turned on the siren for me — *wheee!* I thought that was nice of them.

I spent the next couple of hours in the hospital strapped to that bloody board until they could x-ray me. During that time I thought about how I couldn't even kill myself properly.

A nurse checked on me and asked if I was okay. Sure. Two minutes later, a different nurse came in to check on me. The nurses held my hand. *This is pretty darn good service*, I thought. I often hear people complain about emergency room waiting times, but right now I couldn't see what the fuss was about. I could handle waiting like this. A doctor walked in as well, and she too asked how I was doing. "You know, doc, I'm doing okay."

As the three women were fawning over me, an orderly came in to take me for the x-rays. I told him to take someone else; surely there had to be more urgent cases than a silly old firefighter with a back injury. Not that time. Off I went to the x-ray room, where they took off my bunker pants and boots and placed me on the table with my sweaty gotchies.

As I was lying on the backboard on the x-ray table, Mary walked in. Mary was a damn-good-looking woman I knew from a drop-in centre I visited with my boys. Lo and behold, she was the x-ray tech. Mary told me she saw a lot of her firefighter friends come through the x-ray corridor and she too held my hand to personally make sure I didn't feel alone as they took the pictures.

It turned out that I had muscular damage but no spinal injury. Thank God again. The fire department doctor ordered me to take a couple of months off to fix my back, and fix my head (mostly the latter). My district chief and his aide arrived at the hospital to take me home to my apartment. I couldn't drive, so one of my crewmates, Rob Dies, drove my car home while I rode in the command vehicle.

The house where I was staying was in the High Park section of the city on the opposite side from where my home was with Linda. The apartment was the top floor of a large home with the main floor being the landlord's living quarters. Rob parked my car on one of the side streets, as the house had no parking available for the renters upstairs. The chief and his aide bid me good luck and Rob assisted me up the fire escape to the apartment. It was a slow process. Each step seemed insurmountable. Rob brought me inside and explained my situation to one of the couples that lived there. I thanked Rob, not just for helping me up the stairs, but for not judging me about what my life had become. One of the guys in the apartment led me to the couch and helped me lie down. He didn't know how to get me comfortable. I wouldn't be able to get comfortable for quite some time. He made me a peanut butter sandwich and a cup of tea. I would be resting my back for quite a while, but the healing wouldn't start right away, especially in the mental department.

I had always found writing to be a therapeutic outlet, so I jotted down all the thoughts I was having about depression, and about killing myself. I had thought about hanging myself in the hose tower at work, but when I looked down from the top, I decided I couldn't do that to my friends. I wrote about my regret for messing up the boys' home life and my guilt for actually leaving them. The letter ran about six pages long, and I mailed it to the boys' mother. A lot of the letter was my attempt to defend myself against the crap that spewed out of the Linda's mouth to her family and friends about what a lowlife I was. Maybe *defending* is the wrong word. *Explaining* to them why I was such a lowlife would be more accurate. It felt really good to get it out. I was mending.

32

The Dead Cat Bounce

THERE IS AN EXPRESSION IN the stock-trading world for when a stock plummets, bottoms out, and rises a bit, only to drop again. It's called a "dead cat bounce." My mental feline had taken a face-plant on the sidewalk and was now on a temporary trajectory back up.

Still limping both physically and mentally, I stopped in at the fire hall to say hello to my crew and pick up my paycheque. That's when I learned that a firefighter friend of mine from the hall had committed suicide. He'd shot himself. Right at that point, the cat fell out of the sky and splattered big time on the pavement.

That was too much to handle — way too much. I wandered out of the fire hall and walked for what I'm sure was hours. I called what used to be my home with Linda and the boys to say I was sorry for hurting everyone. There was no answer, and the phone clicked over to voicemail. I said thank you to my ex for trying to get me some help for my depression, but it wasn't working, and I asked her to tell the boys that I loved them. Then I disappeared.

There was a frantic search for me as Linda assumed, by the message left on her voicemail, that I was going to kill myself. At that point I wasn't sure myself.

I WOKE UP ON A bench in one of the city parks along Lake Ontario. Staring straight into the clouds, it reminded me of the aerial battle scenes from one of my favourite war films, *The Battle of Britain*. I thought of the people in wartime London who were losing friends and family members nightly during the Blitz. *Nightly*. And they still kept going, kept on living their daily lives. How had they done it? I realized I had to keep going too. I could keep going. I returned to my apartment.

The fire department doctor got wind of my suicidal thoughts and called me. He was going to commit me to the Clarke Institute of Psychiatry for counselling. *Okay*, I thought, *it's part of my recuperation process*. The next morning I made it to the front door of the Clarke before deciding that I wasn't a nutcase. I turned around and limped home to drink myself into a stupor. Late in the afternoon I received another phone call from the doctor. "Either you show up tomorrow for counselling or I'm going to call the police to come and get you." I apologized for letting him down and promised I'd show up in the morning. I phoned Linda and said I was going to get help. She offered me a lift to the hospital. Mentally at this point I was completely broken and finally capitulated. *You win. I can't survive without you coordinating my life.*

We entered through the admitting door and stepped up to the desk. "I'm Bryan Ratushniak. I'm supposed to see somebody here." She told me to have a seat. Looking at the others in the waiting area, I could almost taste the pain in the room. My whole body felt heavy like I was wearing a suit made out of lead. I was defeated: by Linda, by life. Within a couple of minutes a man ushered me inside to a room. I felt like I had just been pulled into a lifeboat after a shipwreck. I didn't want to leave the hospital. I just wanted a quiet room away from the rest of the world to hide. The doctor said I wasn't going to stay in the hospital overnight but I would see him every day for the first week or so. Linda sat next to me as he explained the process of my rehabilitation. My face was patchy with blotches from the stress. My eyes were red from crying and sleep deprivation. I looked like hell and I knew it.

The doctor read his report from the fire department and asked me a couple of work related questions. I answered the best I could. He knew I had left my marriage and that the woman sitting next to me was the mother of my children.

"How do you envision Linda? How do you see her?" he said.

"I see her like she's a big monster. I'm afraid of her."

"I see," he said. Then Linda patted my knee and leaned in to the doctor. "What he means to say is that the divorce is a big monster."

"Can I have a minute with Bryan?" Clearly, I had an inequitable marriage and I wasn't the personality to stand up to Linda; the woman, as Mom had said, had me under her thumb.

33

The Healing Process

DURING MY RECUPERATION AT THE apartment, I had a lot of time to stew about how messed up my life was. I felt sorry for myself, and imagined that all my happily married friends in Geraldton were laughing at me. I was the guy who went to Toronto to become a big shot. Look at me now, a loser living a student flophouse. I started drinking cheap red wine every day to the point where I could pass out and forget my shitty life. I was also now taking prescribed antidepressants, anti-anxiety medication, and muscle relaxants and painkillers from the fire department doctor to help mend my back.

Kelly, who rented one of the rooms in the house, and I went away for a beach weekend with friends, including some other firefighters. With my immune system fragile from my deteriorated physical and mental condition, I acquired a cough during the weekend and was sipping cough syrup between beers. During the last night I wandered out of the motel room and into the parking lot. It was raining.

Kelly found me leaning up against my car, rubbing my toe in

the dirt, drawing circles over and over again. She approached with caution. "Honey, are you okay?"

"Yeah, I'm fine. I'm just going for a walk."

She went off to get one of the other firefighters to lead me back to bed. I guess the whole antidepressant/muscle relaxant/anti-anxiety/painkiller/cough syrup/alcohol cocktail hadn't sat too well with the low barometric pressure of the rainstorm.

It was a wakeup call — to slow down with the drinking and step back a bit from life, to take a deep breath and all that stuff. Fighting to see your children has got to be the most emotionally taxing endeavour a parent can go through, with the exception of actually losing a child.

IN MY FIRE TRUCK'S RUNNING district there was a public housing complex called Don Mount Court. It's not there anymore, replaced by nicer co-op townhomes. One of the benefits of being on the fire department is getting to work on special holidays when everyone else in the Western world is spending time with their families. (Did you catch the sarcasm there?)

I was missing out on the chance to have Christmas morning with Justin and Michael; getting up early to watch the boys tear into their presents, under our own tree in our own home, like I always envisioned as a new dad. But my opinion of how Christmas was to be didn't matter. I had to have it at Linda's parents' place, an hour-long commute from my work. The boys were really young and I was being deprived of yet another special Christmas memory. In fact for the next two decades I was never to enjoy Christmas morning with my two boys in my own home.

A call came through for Don Mount Court — an alarm had been activated at the complex. We got there and finally found the apartment the alarm had originated from among a maze of townhouses and buildings with the most messed-up numbering system you've ever seen (it was *DaVinci Code*-worthy). On the second floor of the building we discovered that the front window of the apartment had been smashed. Glass covered the ground. The frantic woman inside told us that her estranged husband had tried to break into the apartment and had smashed the window trying to get inside. She'd pulled the fire alarm because, in her words, "The firemen always come."

A couple of our crew chased down the man and grabbed him so the police could arrest the guy. He put up a fight, but Mike Longo, the firefighting/kickboxing bouncer, pinned the guy down and made him squeal like a little pig.

Inside the apartment stood a shivering little boy, still in his pajamas, amid the broken glass and wrapping paper from the morning's Christmas gift opening. His eyes were red and swollen from crying. Here I'd been feeling down because I couldn't be with my boys on Christmas morning, and in front of me there's a terrified little boy the same age as my kids standing in broken glass, the wind howling through the open window.

In short order the rest of the aerial crew placed plastic over the window to keep the heat in. I had a more important duty to perform: tending to the boy. I talked to him, gushing over his new Batman car and trying my best to assure him that things would be all right. It was bullshit. Things were not going to be all right. His dad was going to be tossed in jail and he and his mom would have to be relocated until the window was fixed.

That little boy will relive the terror of that Christmas morning every December 25 for the rest of his life. Christmas memories, I was reminded, are not always so great.

AFTER ABOUT A MONTH OF therapeutic walking in the park I was still in a lot of physical pain. I was feeling sorry for myself because my life had fallen apart, but I pleaded with the fire department doctor to let me back on the trucks. I was feeling lost, without roots. The closest thing to a home was my bed at the hall, I explained.

The doc didn't want me back firefighting yet. He could see I was still sore and kind of messed up in my head, but I persisted. I needed this.

"Okay, but if something happens to you, I'm going to shit on your grave."

My first day back, the place was carpeted in metaphorical eggshells. Everyone was being quiet and polite — not the place that I remembered. Finally, after a few hours of uncomfortable bullshit, my big, bulky friend Barry Locke piped up. "Hey, Rat, you going to snap?"

There was a second or two of silence as everyone waited to see how I would react. I chuckled. It felt good to be made fun of. This was the place I remembered. It felt good to be back home.

One by one the guys would come up to me privately and relay a story that they felt would help me through my crisis. It was clear that I wasn't alone in my emotional turmoil.

Mike Longo, a friend of mine on the pumper, is now retired. He's a short man of Italian heritage who has the gift of gab and is tough as nails. He's a former Canadian kickboxing champion. I used to hold the kick pad for him to train with, and the force of his kicks was so strong that my neck would be stiff for days from the whiplash. He told me a story about when he had first come on the fire department.

"It's like it happened just yesterday," he said. "We went for a suicide, and when we walked into the place a guy was hanging in a closet, dead, a rope around his neck. His two children were tugging on his legs — 'Daddy! Daddy!'" That story kept me alive.

The rest of the crew was really good about letting me work at the hall while I recuperated. When it was my turn to fill in at another station, someone else stepped up and went instead. Damn good guys.

34

"A Boy Fell Out a Third-Floor Window!"

IN PRE-UPGRADE REGENT PARK, MOST of the buildings were cookie-cutter five-storey apartment houses. On one hot summer day, we got a call for a fire in a third-floor apartment. I was driving Aerial 7.

When we arrived, smoke was rolling out the back of the apartment building. Since I was the driver, I stayed with the truck in case they needed to put up the ladder or called for equipment. I helped Gary Christianson, the pumper driver, hook up the hose to the standpipe system, but the crews inside hadn't asked for the lines to be charged yet, so we were standing by waiting for orders.

The radio crackled; the crews inside said they had a hot, working fire. Then there was a scream from one of the residents outside with us — something had happened. Someone yelled over to us that a little boy had jumped out the window to escape the fire.

I thought about my two small boys. This was going to be tough to handle. I didn't want it to be happening; I didn't want a child to die. Gary and I grabbed the first-aid equipment and charged around to the back of the building. On the ground lay a body ... of a dog.

"Oh, it's only a dog," Gary said. We both breathed in, relieved to not be dealing with a dead little boy.

Then we heard a woman scream at us from the crowd. "That's a life! How dare you be so callous! That's someone's family member!" She went on to tell us that she was a lawyer and was going to write a letter to the city saying how disgusted she was.

Instead of telling her to go fuck herself, I bit my tongue. I liked my job. My adrenaline was surging too much for me to come up with a calm response like, *We were just relieved it wasn't a little boy lying there*, or *This job has screwed up my head and emotions so much that the death of a dog just doesn't cut it anymore*. Instead I said nothing.

But I'll say something now: if you are the lawyer who wrote the nasty letter to the mayor about Gary and me in the summer of 1996, *go fuck yourself!*

AROUND THIS TIME I WAS hitting my stride as a firefighter. I was comfortable with my crew and confident that we could tackle any emergency that came our way. After a particularly busy night, I knew I had a full day of parenting ahead of me, as Linda would be off to work and I could finally be with my boys.

At about one o'clock in the morning our truck had a quiet period and I thought it would be a good opportunity to grab forty winks.

But after about ten winks we were dispatched to a fire in a building under construction.

It was an office over a store just down the block from the Rupert Hotel, and it was totally in flames. The building was constructed in the late 1800s, and like buildings of that era, was a tinderbox that could turn into a blaze running the entire length of the block.

Our crews knew this and were extra aggressive on the fire attack. The last thing we wanted was to have fire that took out a whole community. A second alarm was rung. I remember blasts of white light sparking when the aerial tower hit the still energized streetcar lines in front of the building. All crews on scene went the extra mile and held the fire to one building.

After a full night of aggressive firefighting I was happy to see the sun coming up. I knew my shift was almost over. I could go home, have a quick nap, then be semi-rested to take the boys to school.

When we got back to the hall, my relief had not yet made it in. Maybe he was coming in from the other side of the city. As I reached to take off my boots, the alarm went off again. The apparatus doors hadn't closed yet and I stood up to see a column of black smoke rising in the distance. Shit.

We were the first in apparatus on a row of abandoned Victorian townhouses that were designated to be city drop-in centres. Fire was rolling in a room on the second floor.

I was physically and mentally exhausted from busting my ass all night on the second alarm. I'm not sure how effective I would be at this fire but me and another firefighter smashed in the door and took in a hose line.

I made it to the top of the stairs with the aid of the other firefighter from the incoming day shift. He was fresh and eager to attack this fire. I just wanted to curl up and crawl into bed.

It was hot and smoky at the top of the staircase and I couldn't make my way into the room engulfed in flames. No problem. I was happy to wedge myself just inside the doorframe and hit the flames with my hose stream.

Totally exhausted. No energy left. I didn't want to be there. I wanted to be in bed. I turned to the firefighter backing me up to take over. *I'm toast. My shift's done, buddy. I'm sure my relief's here by now*. At that moment a rumble and wave of smoke and fire blew past me. The firefighter backing me up was knocked down the stairs. I was thrown against the doorframe of the room engulfed in fire.

When the smoke cleared, I could see the morning sky where the ceiling used to be.

The roof had collapsed, landing on the floor in front of me, missing me by six inches.

I was so exhausted the severity of the situation didn't even register. It wasn't until later in the day that the shakes came and I realized I had just cheated death again.

35

Locals That Gave the Place Flavour

WHEN I FIRST GOT ON the job, the fire hall doors were never locked — the chief felt it was a public building and should be accessible at all hours of the day. Unfortunately, it was also accessible when the crews were out at a call. It came as no surprise that the TV would go missing on a regular basis, as well any shoes that had been left on the apparatus floor when we went out on a run. That's why the guys at Seven wore the stinkiest beat-up running shoes they could find. At least those would still be there when we got back from picking up another drunk or chasing another false alarm.

Even though my personal life was a mess, I still enjoyed my life at the fire hall. Part of the fun working in Regent Park was the local cast of characters. Here are my favourites:

Frenchie

Frenchie was an interesting character. He would walk by the hall, stick his head in the window, and yell, "Shut your bubble!" for no reason. That's all he ever said. He never talked to anyone or stopped in to say hello. Just "Shut your bubble!" Nobody knows why.

Bagel Ruth

At change of shift on warm nights, the guys would have coffee in
the parking lot and wait for Nick the Ice-Cream Man. One night
a street guy walked by with a monstrous plastic bag jammed full of
bagels — a couple hundred for sure.

I, being the smartass that I am, yelled out to ask if he had any
lox to go with that bale o' bagels. The guy dropped the bag, reached
inside, and started whipping bagels at me. I was like Ken Dryden
trying to stop a barrage of pucks blasted my way by the Soviets.
I was laughing so hard I spilled coffee all over my legs. After he'd
pelted us with thirty or forty bagels, he just walked off, never to
be seen again.

The bagels were gone by next morning, and I had to spend
about an hour hosing seagull shit off the cars.

Trish the Dish

Trish the Dish was a firefighter groupie who had been making the
rounds for a couple of decades. I only met her once. She was sitting
in the floor-watch room when I arrived for work one afternoon.
The guys were all jammed into the kitchen because nobody wanted
to talk to her. She seemed nice to me.

Trish died a few years ago. Her obituary was pinned in a promi-
nent position on the station bulletin board and someone added the
handwritten words *Trish the Dish is dead*. The flags were lowered.

Brian the Artist

Brian was a First Nations artist whose paintings hung in galler-
ies around the world. He had a ton of talent, but loved the bottle a bit too much. He would sell the guys art at cut-rate prices
when he was sober, asking for cash so he could get torqued. There
were a couple of legitimate art collectors in the hall; Brian would
sketch something on a piece of paper and sell it to one of the guys
for ten bucks. He tried selling me a chalk sketch he put on our
blackboard, but one of the guys told me I was getting ripped off.

Because our doors were always unlocked, Brian once stumbled in when the truck was out on a call, pissed on our couch, and tried phoning for pizza on the department phone: a direct line to dispatch.

Gail the Hooker
Back in the day, prostitutes used to have to check in at the police station next door to the fire hall, so we got to know a lot of familiar faces. It was always a good time. A sex worker advocate once came to talk to us about supporting the prostitutes working the streets. She gave out stickers that I put on my guitar case — the one with the bear teeth marks in it — that said "Support sex workers" and "A hooker's a person in your neighbourhood."

A regular, Gail, always said hi to us. One day she came into the hall to grab a couple of the latex gloves we used for medical calls, saying that she had run out of condoms.

Lance Armstrong Wannabe
There's a sign on the back of every fire truck: stay back 150 metres (in the States it says to stay back 200 feet). There's a reason those things are affixed to the backs of fire trucks. During an emergency run, the drivers of these fifty-ton trucks have to weave back and forth through traffic dodging a-holes who don't pull over, all the while keeping a lookout for the address they're responding to and trying to spot a fire hydrant behind illegally parked cars so they can have water to put out the friggin' fire they're about to arrive at.

Our Lance Armstrong wannabe decided to race his bicycle behind our pumper as it was responding to an alarm call. He was decked out like a Tour de France force of one: tight jersey, spacey helmet, skimpy riding shorts — *the whole shebang*. This guy was really motoring. We were breaking traffic for Lance and he was drafting behind our truck like a Formula One racer. His head was tucked down and he was cranking those pedals at lightning speed when we reached our emergency — and stopped. He didn't. BAM!!! Lance ate the back of our fire truck.

Lance was actually a yuppie lawyer only playing at being a cycle star. He sued the fire department for damaging his bicycle.

Johnny the Walker

J.W. was a man who stole hand sanitizer from hospitals to get drunk. Fortunately for him, the SARS outbreak in Toronto meant that all public buildings had to install hand sanitizer dispensers at their doors to combat the spread of the virus. While SARS is long gone, the dispensers remained, even before they became far more common during the COVID-19 crisis. J.W. would just walk through the front door, break open the dispenser, and walk off with the bag of sanitizer goo, which he'd suck on like a freezie treat. It goes without saying that this messed him up good. He would end up in the hospital almost daily. A paramedic we worked with said he was admitted more than two hundred times in less than a year.

At the rate he was drinking the stuff, we didn't think he was long for this world.

One night our crews answered a call for a pedestrian hit by a delivery truck, and found J.W. folded up under the vehicle. He was taken to hospital. Two weeks later, the paramedics that we ran with said he was still alive. His back was broken, but he was alive.

Months later we heard through the grapevine that J.W. had gone MIA. He'd slipped out of the hospital with his walker and cervical collar. We got another call for Mr. Invincible a month later, sans walker and collar, but still stealing and drinking hand sanitizer.

After dealing with him for two years, I finally asked him why he drank that sanitizer gunk. He replied that his ex-wife had accused him of sexually assaulting his child and he couldn't see him anymore. He was going to commit suicide by drinking himself to death.

Every tragedy has a story. Every whack job — and I'm including myself in that category — has a reason for their actions. It was easy to become inured to the street people we dealt with on a daily basis, but to stop myself from going crazy (or at least crazier), it was better to keep a safe distance and just tackle the symptoms.

36

Getting Married

I WAS ACCEPTING MY LOT in life with my limited space in the apartment and wished I could magically fast forward through the depressive months, perhaps years, and get to a time when I would feel better. Kelly and I began dating and she tried her best to nurse me back to health. She wasn't sure how to help with someone suffering from depression, but she knew creating a home environment for my next uncertain chapter of life would help to relieve some of the depressive pressure on me. Kelly was also sensitive to my situation with regards to getting access to Justin and Michael and helped me to buy books, toys, and a puppet stage to create an inviting environment for the boys' visits with Dad. I took photos to show the safe and loving space for the boys to visit, but still, Linda wouldn't let me see them. Needless to say I still struggled mentally because I wanted to see my children and was being denied access to them by their mother for the exact same reason. It was a catch-22 situation. Linda declared sole parental custody of Justin and Michael, arguing that I wasn't emotionally stable enough to share in the parenting duties. Considering my history of being a patient at the Clarke Institute and that statistically fathers face an uphill battle in family court, my lawyer said to forget even trying for shared custody. It wasn't going to happen. He suggested that I just seek regular access to the boys.

I took this challenge on with vigour. I knew I wasn't crazy and I was just feeling depressed because I couldn't see my boys. Surely it was a cut and dry situation and once the court saw I wasn't an unfit father I would be able to see my kids again. At the fire hall I asked my crewmates if they could write a personal reference of a short paragraph or two saying they've known me for a while; that I wasn't crazy; and that they saw me interact with my boys and felt I was a good father. Then, expanding my scope I asked my former neighbours for references, since they would have seen me the most when I took the kids to the park and school. In total I collected over thirty personal references to show to family court that I was a good dad.

After a prolonged legal fight between our respective lawyers, with no quarter given on the access front, our case ended up in court. The judge appeared fed up with the deadlock and she asked my lawyer what I was seeking as far as parental access. He turned to me and asked how much access I was looking for. After not seeing the boys for five months I said, "Anything." With that, the judge, considering the well-being of the boys and their need to see their father, stated, "We'll start with six hours of supervised access a week."

"That's too much!" shouted Linda, which was received by the judge with a scowl.

Slowly I was reintroduced into the boys' lives with either Linda or a doctor she and the boys were seeing as supervisors.

Over the next several weeks when my visits became more frequent — six hours a week, nine hours a week, and so on — life became better. Even at the fire hall, I felt happier. It wasn't the perfect situation, having to endure a condescending stare from

Linda or some other supervisor she had reluctantly approved, but it was a lot better than it was when I was staring at the walls wondering if I could endure the pain of missing my boys.

Eventually Justin and Michael were allowed to have an overnight stay at the apartment. We watched movies and played games. Over the next several months the boys adapted to the new normal wonderfully.

Kelly took on her role as dad's partner and stepmom well. She used to be a summer camp counsellor as a teenager and had a knack for coming up with entertaining activities for our new family. I was starting to feel less like a loser and more "normal." I learned to compartmentalize the stress of dealing with Linda and enjoy the next chapter in life with a new loving partner and accepted that I'd been relegated to an arm's-length father. Kelly and I got married in the autumn of 1995.

I WAS NOW PHYSICALLY HEALTHY, my children were happy and healthy, and I had a long career, on a job I loved, ahead of me, and a new wife. Life was good. Or at least, it should have been. In reality, I was putting on a mask when dealing with people I thought were better than me. Being with Kelly meant being in her social world. I was trying to fit in. To adjust to my new life. To heal. But I still felt like an outsider with Kelly's friends. Being an introvert, my entire social circle consisted of the men and women on the fire department that I worked with or family and friends from my hometown in Northwestern Ontario. By contrast, Kelly was an extrovert and had friends from high school, university, and work she socialized with, most of whom were of a more academic background than me.

Many of Kelly's friends had assumed she would go out with an intellect; she couldn't possibly be with a man who didn't at least get into university, let alone have a degree or doctorate in something. I was trying to interact with men in suits, intellects, people who were well-travelled and well-read. At parties I would chat with anyone, trying to convince myself I was worthy of their interest, but I always thought they were looking down their nose at me, the firefighter.

37

The House on Balmoral

IN 1997, AFTER I LEFT Regent Park, I went to the mid-town section of the city for a bit. I had been promoted to acting captain, but since there was already an acting captain on my truck, I got bumped — to a slow truck. It was an aerial like the one I was on in Regent Park, but I was back in a neighbourhood of the same kind of rich folks I had started the job with.

The first few months were great. I would spend my shifts sitting in the cozy fire hall, drinking a cup of tea and listening to the boys in the core of the city freezing their asses off all night. The neighbourhood clientele were an upscale bunch and even the name of the street the fire hall was on, Balmoral, had a touch of class to it. There were no skanks yelling at us, no hookers with clients in the parking lot. The only people we encountered were well-groomed, well-mannered, and sporting a full set of teeth. At one point, after dropping off donations for the food bank at the Balmoral station, a neighbourhood group raised money to buy the fire hall new couches, since ours were (as in all fire halls) held together with duct tape and sported soup cans for legs.

It was all too ... nice. There were no whack jobs starting

fistfights with us, no drunks throwing beer bottles. The neighbours at home noticed that my wacky work stories had stopped. And now that I was back in the world of polite people with jobs, I hated it. The lack of craziness, I mean. The guys I worked with, though, were awesome and I went on to forge lifelong friendships with them. But there would be no shit hitting the fan anytime soon, and to be honest, it turns out that I like shit-showering fans.

Still, I enjoyed my time at the Balmoral hall. The place had a rich history, including a couple of haunting stories. Literally — the place had a ghost. I never saw him, but I wanted to. The fire hall was built in 1911, and it would creak a bit at night; you really couldn't blame that on the ghost. But, on more than one occasion, a captain working in the front room of Station 24 was greeted by a man with the tall fire hat and long beard that firefighters had worn at the turn of the previous century. Apparently he would just stand in the room and stare, making sure you were doing your job. I never figured out if the stories were true or just the result of a firefighter with the jitters.

I told this story to a man who once managed a couple of nineteenth-century walk-ups down the street from the fire hall that had housed Irish immigrant women — usually nurses who worked in Toronto — when they were built. He sort of went pale. When he was the superintendent of the two buildings, on more than one occasion he had seen the ghostly figure of a woman in a long red cape walking past him or through the room where he was staying. I thought that was cool. Both the fire station and the apartment buildings backed onto the same cemetery, the one where Mary Pickford, Hollywood's sweetheart, was laid to rest. Could that be the source of the spooky happenings?

I NEVER SAW A REAL ghost during my time at Balmoral, but I did see a guy who should have been one. A few months into my new posting, we answered a call for a pedestrian struck by a car. When we arrived, it was clear that this person had hopped off a streetcar into the path of a fast-travelling Jeep Cherokee and was now squished underneath it. One leg of the victim was sticking out over the driver's front wheel and the rest of the poor guy was twisted under the truck, face down. The front of the Jeep was caved in.

I jumped off the rig and looked for the tell-tale sign of trauma, a pool of blood. I bent down and looked under the truck. At that point the dude squished up underneath said to me, "My shoulder kinda hurts." Holy shit! I stumbled backwards and stained my undies as if I'd just spoken to a ghost. What the hell? That guy should have been dead!

The rescue squad arrived with the department mechanic on board (he happened to be at the hall and had just come along for the ride to see what was going on). After the squad had stabilized the truck, the mechanic took off the tire and the squad crew used airbags and jacks to lift the Jeep off the guy. All he had suffered was a sore shoulder and some scraped knuckles. He was the luckiest guy I had ever seen in my life. I smiled at him as he was taken off to the hospital.

FOR ME, 1997 TURNED OUT to be at the extreme opposite end of the happiness chart compared to just two years before, when I had been ready to end it all. My home life was moving along nicely: My marriage was going well and I was getting to spend time with my boys on a regular basis. They were both well-adjusted and excelling at school. That being said, I needed a change. My personal life was back on track, but I wanted to get the zing back in my professional life. I knew that if I was transferred to a busier truck it meant I would most likely be confronted with more traumatic situations than if I stayed on a slower apparatus. But mentally I felt better and convinced myself I was cured of my episode of stress. I defined myself as a firefighter to my friends and neighbours and felt a greater sense of worth relaying the dramatic events of the job. The crazier the story, the greater the sense of worth. In my mind I was ready to get back into the heavy action.

38

A Much Needed Change

I PUT IN FOR A transfer to a busier truck in the downtown core; about a year later, I was shifted to the busiest fire truck in Canada.

Toronto amalgamated with its five surrounding cities and boroughs in 1998. Etobicoke, York, East York, North York, and Scarborough had now become part of the City of Toronto. With a total of eighty-three fire stations divided into four commands — north, south, east, and west — the newly renamed Toronto Fire Services became the fifth largest fire department in North America. All the fire apparatus across the city were renumbered to create a unified fire department. My new truck, Pumper 3, was renumbered Pumper 314 (Command 3, District 1, Station 4).

Pumper 314 — the busiest fire truck in Canada, running about 4,700 emergency calls a year — ran the Yonge Street strip in Toronto.

Yonge Street is lined with stores and restaurants. At one time it was shut down and turned into a pedestrian boulevard as an experiment. It didn't stick, though; people still wanted to cruise the strip. Traffic can get to be bumper-to-bumper during prime cruising hours.

Driving an emergency vehicle in those conditions takes a bit of nerve and skill. Even with the siren blaring, lights flashing, and air horn blasting, people don't give a damn about a fire truck rushing to an emergency, because they themselves are rushing home to watch *American Idol* or *The Voice* on the tube.

During a response to a medical emergency southbound on Yonge Street, both southbound lanes were plugged with traffic, so we crossed the centreline into the northbound lanes, which for the moment were clear because all oncoming traffic was stopped at a red light down the block.

As we motored south in the northbound lanes, a teenage girl listening to an iPod/phone darted through the stopped traffic, oblivious to our siren and deafening air horn.

A woman on the sidewalk screamed. The truck locked up its brakes and screeched sideways to a stop, creating skid marks and a cloud of smoke. It came to rest so close to the girl that her long red hair actually swiped the mirror on the captain's side.

"Jesus Christ, you could have been killed!" Captain Billy said to her. He was really shaken up.

The girl cursed at him. I took her by the shoulders, marched her to the sidewalk, and pulled out her earbuds.

"I said I was sorry. Duh!" she told me.

I jumped back on the truck. When we got to the location we'd been dispatched to, it turned out to be one of our regular drunks. He told us to fuck off. I was still on an adrenaline peak from almost seeing a girl get killed, so I launched into him. "We almost killed someone on the way here to pick up your sorry ass!"

39

Pinup Boy

A YEAR AFTER WE MARRIED, Kelly and I bought a home in the west end of Toronto and I really started to feel that I was on the road to recovery, mentally speaking. I began to embrace the social outings with Kelly's friends.

At social functions, barbeques, or dinner parties, when women found out that I was a Toronto firefighter, they would always ask if I was in the calendar. Yes, I was … back in the 1900s. Not only that, I was one of the *Toronto Sun*'s "Sunshine Boys" — a daily feature with a beefcake photo of a local resident. Not once, but twice!

The first Sunshine Boy appearance came as a result of my bodybuilding. At the risk of appearing too humble, I have to say that I used to be a fairly good-looking man. During the 1990s most of my off time was spent in the gym working out, chasing my dream of one day becoming Mr. Canada: Champion Bodybuilder. I was making my way up the ranks to where I was at the provincial level of competition — a big step up from the beer-league bodybuilding competitions I had been competing in.

Back in 1990, to promote the upcoming Provincial Championships, the first provincial level competition in which I was to compete, the organizers teamed up with the *Sun* to feature some of the contenders, and I was asked to participate.

The shoot was a quick, efficient affair in a downtown photo studio where I was made to pose like I was casually ripping off my Bodybuilding Ontario tank top to show my rock hard abs. My brother Adrian said that when he was a fire inspector at Canada's Wonderland, the resulting Sunshine Boy photo was pinned up on the bulletin board in the fire prevention office by the girls in the office.

It was a good way to help promote bodybuilding, but resulted in the inevitable ribbing when I arrived at the fire hall for my next shift. "Rat, Rat, Rat, you'll never live it down," I was told.

But it wasn't my last time as a Sunshine Boy. The next time, it was for the benefit of firefighters.

It came as no surprise to me that when the subject of a charity calendar featuring Toronto firefighters was broached, the committee suggested me as one of the models. My ego would accept nothing less. Especially after the Sunshine Boy ribbing I'd had to endure.

The Toronto Fire Department had never done a calendar before. If you have ever seen the spectacle that is a calendar competition, you know it can be, shall we say, cheesy — certainly not becoming to a career firefighter in the city of Toronto. But a new regime was in the "Big House" after the city amalgamated with its five surrounding municipalities in 1998, and they didn't think it was unbecoming. Cheesy or not, we were going to have a calendar.

Firefighters don't participate in these things for the sake of vanity. Calendars raise a lot of money for charity. And there's no shortage of willing firefighters ready to step up to the plate for a chance to help raise money for a worthy cause, whether it be a charity for Muscular Dystrophy research or, in this case, cancer research at Princess Margaret Hospital in Toronto.

Montreal had called up Toronto to suggest combining our two charities and coproducing a calendar. The Montreal people had already shot six portraits and they asked Toronto to contribute the same.

MY SHOOT TOOK PLACE IN the apparatus bay an hour before I was to start night shift, standing on a makeshift set dressed up with fire extinguishers and axes. The lights were adjusted. Polaroids were shot to get the colour and lighting just right. I was a competitive bodybuilder at the time, so I did my best to pump up my pecs and pipes for the photographer. I did that by eating dried fruit to carb up and puff out my muscles, but I ate too much; it gave me cramps.

They needed something to highlight my physique — body oil — but I had forgotten to bring any. I had dropped the ball, but my fire hall brothers, wanting to help out, dug under the kitchen sink for the jug of old vegetable oil we used to fill the deep fryer. I smelled like fish and chips, but I looked great. I was Mr. October. To promote the calendar, images — including mine — were printed as Sunshine Boys by the *Sun*, and that's how I made my second appearance in that feature.

The calendar-signing appearances were phenomenal. Women went nuts! It didn't matter if you were in shape or good-looking, as long as you wore your fire duds. Hell, even Elmer Fudd could have gotten laid if he wore suspenders and a fire hat.

Women went crazy at the signing appearances. I felt as if I were Michael Bublé, Donny Osmond, or Guy Lombardo, depending on the age of the woman who wanted her calendar signed. Most guys signed their name with a suggestive cliché. *I'm hot for you*, signed Bernie. *I'll make you wet*, signed Jed. The women loved it.

I tried my best to be original with each calendar. The lineups were long and we had to keep things moving; there really wasn't a lot of time for originality. Since I was signing literally hundreds of them, it wasn't long before I started doing the whole cliché thing myself: *You burn me up. I'll ride the pole for you.* And those were my best ones. Some didn't even make sense, come to think of it. *You're so good-looking, you take my cramps away* comes to mind. The fluorescent lighting in the malls was starting to cook my brain.

Many men came by as well to buy calendars for themselves or as a gift for their partner. Some women bought them for their gay son or brother. Good — a break from the assembly-line sentiments I was spewing for the better part of a week leading up to Christmas.

A co-worker — let's call him Peewee — arrived at one of the signings. He wanted me to sign a calendar for a gay family friend who was a chef in an upscale restaurant. He said the chef thought Mr. October was the best-looking hose boy of the bunch. I did my best to be sincere. After all, this was a very well respected chef in a very chichi restaurant. So Mr. October signed *To Charles: BONE APPETIT*. My yellowing image is still taped in a couple of lockers across the city.

40

You're Never Alone

MAPLE LEAF GARDENS WAS A Depression-era project that became the focal point of Toronto entertainment for seventy-five years. It was home to eleven Stanley Cup champion Toronto Maple Leafs teams, and the site of Bill Barilko's goal, which the rock group The Tragically Hip wrote about in their song "Fifty Mission Cap." The Gardens was host to a screaming horde in 1966 when the Beatles took the stage. My gym teacher from high school in Geraldton was there and remarked later, "You couldn't hear a goddamned note because of all the screaming."

Because of its long and distinguished history, the Gardens was deemed a historical landmark. But in 2004, it was empty, a victim of its age waiting for its fate to be decided. The choice at the time was between a Home Depot or a Loblaws grocery store.

Every couple of months we would get a call for alarm bells ringing in the Gardens. I was acting captain of the first-arriving apparatus on one such call, so it was up to my crew and me to check things out and determine the cause of the alarm.

The Gardens is a big building with a maze of backrooms, but the onsite staff were generally pretty good about directing us to the affected zones. Most of the time it was a far-off supply room or office where the window was broken. During the winter it was cold enough to freeze the sprinkler pipes in the unheated building, which would set off the alarms. But this time it was summer, and my money was on a cause other than frozen pipes; I knew that the pipes weren't frozen on a steamy August afternoon, and that the activated detector was in the rink area.

The empty building was in a state of decay. Only a few security lights were on in the quiet, cavernous space; I was glad the security guard had turned them on, because I get spooked in the dark. Our crew walked out into the semidarkness, lighting the way with our flashlights. I shone my light up into the stands to see if we could figure out why the alarm had gone off. The beam lit up the face of a dead man. Then another, and another.

The lights came up. We were surrounded by the dead eyes of thousands of Depression-era ghosts sitting silently in the stands, staring at us. If my sphincter hadn't puckered up just then, I think I would have crapped my pants. There was a boxing ring in the middle of the rink. We were standing in Madison Square Garden in the 1930s.

Something's wrong here, I thought, showing incredible insight. The security guy came over and said we were standing in part of the set for the Ron Howard/Brian Grazer/Penny Marshall film *Cinderella Man*, starring Russell Crowe and Renée Zellweger.

Twelve thousand inflated dummies dressed in period costumes sat in the stands, filled out the background for the boxing scenes. "They're cheaper than extras," the security guard said. "They're always on time, they don't bitch, and you don't have to feed them. Although they don't respond to direction very well."

But the reason for the fire alarm was still to be determined. My first task was to crawl into the boxing ring and raise my arms over my head in triumph as I addressed the silent hordes. I couldn't resist the opportunity to be a goof.

Eventually I found the cause, don't recall what it was, and radioed dispatch to clear all the other trucks at the call.

Not only did I have the crap scared out of me inside Maple Leaf/ Madison Square Garden(s), we had created a traffic jam outside. The city was replacing the streetcar tracks and our truck was blocking the only open lane so my driver drove the truck up onto the sidewalk to let the other vehicles pass and the flow of traffic start up again. I thanked the security guard for his help and walked back to the truck, rearranging my damp underwear on the way. I jumped into the cab of the truck, and told the driver to hightail it back to the barn. He gave a little tip-of-the-hat salute and signalled to the pedestrians on the sidewalk to move their asses so we wouldn't run them over. About a second after the truck started moving, it started to sink then stopped with a thud. It had gone through a hydro grate, a metal grid over a below-ground electrical vault. The front wheels ended up below street level, the back end in the air. I don't think the truck even stopped rocking before cellphone cameras came out by the dozen.

41

A Hotshot Firefighter

IT TAKES ABOUT TWO SECONDS to make an initial evaluation of an emergency scene. I knew instinctively if an incident or fire was going to escalate or not. Still, I could never completely account for factors I either couldn't see or didn't know about. What time of day was it? With a fire in a residential building at three o'clock in the morning, there was a good chance people were sleeping inside, while an office building at the same time of night was probably empty. But I could never be sure. Had a burglar torched the place and was now caught inside? What colour was the smoke? Was it black, white, or grey? Was it wafting out lazily or rolling out under pressure? Was it yellowish brown? Was a backdraft imminent?

Dumpster fires were a fairly routine call. Most of the time they're started by some smoker tossing in a cigarette and setting the trash on fire. In high-rise buildings the garbage compactor and attached Dumpster catch fire on a regular basis. Smokers — a.k.a. firefighters' job security — empty their ashtrays before the butts are completely out and set the entire garbage-chute system on fire. Lots of smoke and a pain in the ass, but no real damage.

One day when I was acting captain, we got another Dumpster fire call. The bin was already outside when someone set it on fire, either accidently or for kicks. It was well away from the building, just a Dumpster burning on its own.

When we arrived, a distraught woman was pointing to the Dumpster, which was blowing flames about ten feet into the air. It looked spectacular, like a burning tank in a war flick. Cool, but routine.

The distraught woman ran up to the truck, the flames roaring just behind her. In my best butterscotch customer-service-at-the-Ritz voice, I asked, "So, what seems to be the problem here?"

In a split second her expression changed from *Oh my God, there's a fire!* to *Are you a complete idiot? There's a fire!* to *Hey, asshole, just put out the fire.*

You gotta love working downtown.

BEING IN A BUSY FIRE station on a busy truck had been my dream once I knew in my heart I wanted to be a firefighter. I wanted to help people. I wanted the excitement of the job. I wanted to work the biggest fires, be part of the most dramatic rescues. To earn the admiration of the people and the respect of my fellow firefighters. I wanted to feel worthy. I wanted to do good. But sometimes you fail.

On a cool autumn morning I was relieving on a pumper in the Cabbagetown neighbourhood of downtown Toronto, just outside of my normal running area. A mix of beautiful Victorian homes and low-rise rental apartments. We were dispatched to a fire in a low-rise apartment building on Sherbourne Street.

We arrived with no smoke showing from the street side of the building. We were directed to a fire on the second floor at the end of a long hallway. Thick black smoke was pushing out around an apartment door. We masked up and I knocked in the door. The other two in my crew took in a hose line and I did a search as we advanced the line to the back of the apartment to where the living room was burning. The building was built around the 1930s or '40s, and had large apartments finished with hardwood floors and solid wood doors. With the thick black smoke, my visibility was zero. I would have to do a search by feel. I held on to the hose line and ran my hand against the wall, looking for doors that would lead to a bedroom where, at this early hour, the tenant could be sleeping. Once inside the apartment I felt what I thought was a narrow closet door. In my mind I envisioned a linen closet. I continued down the hall, dragging the hose with one hand and feeling the walls for a door. I felt an opening and went in the room to do a quick sweep, looking for victims. It was the kitchen. All clear. I moved back out to the hall and followed the hose line to the living room area where my crewmates were knocking down the flames. I turned over a few pieces of furniture to help extinguish the last smouldering fire. By this time our low-air alarms began to sound. Our crew exited the building, handing over the hose line to another crew, to get a refill on our air cylinders.

After getting a fresh cylinder and a quick drink of water I walked back into the building. As I approached the steps a medic crew were carrying out a soot-covered man on a stretcher. Where the hell did he come from?

The victim was experiencing agonal breathing. This desperate gasping for air is usually a sign that the heart is no longer pumping oxygenated blood. The man was dying. I rushed back into the apartment. By this time the smoke had cleared a bit and I could see the layout of the apartment: a long hallway, rooms on the right leading to the living room where the fire was. The first door on the right was a bathroom. What I'd thought was simply a linen closet was actually the bathroom that sheltered the man from the fire. I could see the smudge from my glove as it ran across the wall during my search. I went into the bathroom. The entire room was blackened by smoke. An outline on the floor under the sink told the story of the man's desperate attempt to survive.

At the time of the fire he was probably caught in the bathroom. The heavy smoke, from the burning vinyl records in the living room, made his escape impossible. Once enveloped in the lethal smoke he had crawled under the sink, placing his head over a bucket of water in his attempt to breathe. Neither our crew nor the second crew found the man until the smoke had cleared enough to spot him tucked under the sink. Footprints in the sooty floor showed the path of a firefighter walking right past the man on his way to open a window to vent the smoke.

I didn't know how to act. I didn't know how to feel. I talked to one of the firefighters in the second crew. He said, trying assuage my anxiety, "Christ, nobody saw him. How the hell were you to know he was curled up under the sink?" I didn't know. But I didn't open the door either. The door I thought was a linen closet. The man survived thanks to the paramedics and hospital staff. It was a story, years later, I relayed to a television crew filming for a show called *Life Story Project* in a segment on "Failures, Mistakes, and Triumphs." This was a failure of mine. It makes me ill just to write about.

BY THE TIME I WAS transferred to the core of the city to 314, I was doing well in my acting endeavours, making a good buck appearing in commercials. It seemed that my face was always on TV. The guys and I were sitting in the fire hall one day when — oh, looky here! — we saw the Rat doing a McDonald's commercial, followed by the Rat doing a LePage's caulking spot. People would recognize me as "that guy" or ask if they knew me from somewhere. Sometimes they would declare outright, "You're that guy!" if they recognized me from a popular commercial.

In August 2001, I had scored a spot for Budweiser that was going to be broadcast in the US and the UK. The coin I would potentially make from that one gig could be in the tens of thousands of dollars. In the commercial I played a firefighter cooking hot dogs, only to have a Dalmatian jump up and steal one — again, art at its highest level. And since it was shot at a real-life fire hall and I was a real-life firefighter, I got consulting fees as well.

At this point, nothing could spoil my awesome life. I was walking around with a perpetual smile. With the royalty cheques about to flow in, Kelly and I went on a shopping spree and booked a cruise to take the boys to the Caribbean. Then, three weeks after the commercial was filmed, I got a nice blue letter from Anheuser-Busch saying they were cancelling the whole campaign. Bryan wasn't getting any royalty cheques. Shit! I had just spent a crap-load on furniture and a family cruise. How could things get worse?

A couple of days later, on September 11, the entire world changed.

In the days immediately following the tragedy on September 11, 2001, the brotherhood of firefighters was never stronger, at least in my memory. Watching the events unfold on CNN felt like seeing my family members getting killed. I still feel a deep sickness in my belly when I think about the loss.

Here in Toronto, American flags flew on all the fire trucks as a tribute to our lost brothers. People stood in the streets and saluted as we responded to fire calls. Emotionally, it was very painful. As firefighters, we wanted to be there in New York to save our brothers. We felt their fear as they realized their fate. Those men and women ran into the Twin Towers knowing that it was futile, like parents who can't swim jumping into a river to save their drowning child. God bless them all.

The world changed after 9/11. It changed the minute the first plane smashed into the World Trade Center. But firefighting protocols are firmly set; it takes time to change them. Immediately after I saw the second tower come down on CNN, I phoned the fire hall to see how the guys were making out. Everyone was kind of stunned and nervous. *What's going to happen now? Is this World War Three?* I asked what directives had come down from headquarters. I was told the guys were to make sure the doors were locked but the upper management was scrambling, not knowing really what the hell to do. We'd never faced a situation like this before.

The American flags stayed on all the fire trucks for months. Not officially, of course, but because the brothers and sisters would spontaneously drape flags and black shrouds across the fronts of the trucks. Some people would give us grief for flying American flags on our trucks; they said we should be ashamed of supporting an unjust war. But it had nothing to do with George W. in the White House. We were in mourning.

42

Merry Effing Christmas

IN 2003 I TURNED FORTY, and Kelly arranged a surprise party at my local pub. It was a grand time, with much of my crew from Station 24 and my new hall, 314, in attendance. I even got a surprise visit from my sister Brenda (whose clothes I hadn't worn in years) and her husband, Donny. It was great to see them, and even more so because I knew the drive from Geraldton took fourteen hours.

Two weeks later, Donny was dead from a heart attack. He was only forty-six. Two weeks after that, my mom died from congestive heart failure. Three weeks after that, my dad died from complications due to a stroke. As years go, 2003 sucked.

In the aftermath, Chereyl, Brenda, Adrian, and I became closer than ever. We had come together to deal with the burial arrangements and sorting out of the estates. We had never been a very emotionally demonstrative family, but this series of losses changed that. I was hurting emotionally, but luckily I could count on the strength and support of my beautiful wife, Kelly.

The following winter, Kelly left me. Before everything turned to shit, I guess life had been going too well for me. Maybe I was due for a metaphorical kick in the balls. I moved into my brother's place, an hour outside the city, while our matrimonial home was up for sale. I was drowning in a sea of expenses, trying to save for first and last months' rent for a new apartment, child support, my boys' university education, a divorce lawyer, and subsequent division of the assets, all the while paying for a new car that I had leased just the previous spring. I was running a deficit, and every month I was getting deeper and deeper in debt. Eventually the banks refused me any more credit. The winter of 2004 was going to see one bleak Christmas.

On Christmas Eve, I got a phone call at work. A young female voice was on the other end. "Hey, Bryan, I was hoping to get in touch with you. Are you going to be around the fire hall for a bit?"

I told her yes, that we tend to stay at the fire hall when we're working, but also that we could be at any number of addresses up and down the core of the city.

A half hour later there was a knock at the door at 314 and I opened it. A good-looking woman was standing there. She asked for me, and I started thinking that I might have seen her on set sometime and maybe she wanted to talk about TV work and agents and that sort of thing — it wouldn't be the first time.

"Hey, it's Christmas Eve. Come on in and warm up a bit," I said, trying to be charming.

"You're probably expecting these," she replied. She handed me an envelope and bolted out the door. I opened the envelope and discovered that I had just been served my divorce papers. On Christmas Eve.

That night at 314 was as busy as usual. The gay bar next to the hall was pounding techno music and rowdy a-holes were yelling and fighting in the alley. I stewed in my room at the station between calls, replaying the past six months of my life.

THE NEXT MORNING, EXHAUSTED FROM running my ass off all night, I trudged outside into the snow. A full beer bottle had been smashed across the top on my new car, denting the roof and cover-ing my overpriced vehicle with frozen Budweiser. Of course it had to be Budweiser! As if it weren't enough that they had dumped me from the commercial that triggered my spending spree in antici-pation of the thousands in royalties that didn't come — the main source of my massive credit card debt — their frozen product now shrouded my once oh-so-perfect life with shame. *Why me? What have I done to deserve this? How come my life sucks so much?*

Twenty-four hours later, the problems that had made me feel so sorry for myself came splashing into perspective. A tsunami struck the Indian Ocean on Boxing Day, killing more than 230,000 people in fourteen countries. What I had perceived as catastrophe in my personal life was nothing compared to the death and destruc-tion experienced by the millions affected by the giant tidal wave.

I looked in the mirror and convinced myself that I had nothing to complain about. Perspective is everything, just like when I felt suicidal in 1994 and started thinking about the British people enduring night after night of bombing in the Second World War. I could endure this.

I envisioned all the negative things in my life, whether it was my marriage breakup or my financial problems, as a kind of swamp I had been dropped into. The only way to get out of a situation like that is to keep walking forward until you get to the edge, find some solid ground, and then, once your feet are dry, order a shitload of chicken wings and beer.

I struggled, but I kept on moving forward. "Forward only! Forward only!" was my mantra. "Life is a one-way street."

After a few months, things were finally getting a little better in my personal life and I was starting to feel good about myself again. I even briefly dated a beautiful television personality I had met at a charity event. She found me charming, cute, and funny, but ultimately sad inside. She became a good friend and convinced me that I wasn't ready to see anyone romantically just yet. She was very supportive and let me know that a lot of wonderful things awaited me in life. Sadly, that didn't include a romantic relationship with her.

While still dealing with the divorce elements and subsequent financial burden, I had moved into a two-bedroom apartment back in the east end of Toronto so I could be closer to the boys and they could have their own room when they stayed overnight. It was much too expensive for me but it forced me to work harder at getting back on my feet.

To trim some expenses to help with my ability to pay my rent, I got rid of the expensive car and bought a cheap, beat-up Volvo. A firefighter from the Yorkville Fire Hall knew I needed an extra job and offered some of his work as a bottled water delivery driver. The commercial auditions and the prospect of a television windfall had dried up and I readily accepted. It wasn't going to be easy on my body as I was training hard for the upcoming Canadian Bodybuilding Championships and I still had to fit in gym time if I had any chance of getting in competition condition. There would be limited down-time between fire hall tours of duty.

On my days off from the fire hall, and when I was in delivery driver mode, I would leave my apartment at six in the morning, drive to the far west end of the city, pick up the delivery truck, drive back into the core of the city for a full day's hard work slugging fifty-pound bottles, drive back out to the west end in rush hour traffic, drop off the truck, jump in my Volvo, drive back across the city through rush hour traffic to my apartment, walking in the door around half past seven in the evening. It paid $150 per day.

When I worked the night shift at 314 I would leave the fire hall at seven in the morning, after doing fifteen, twenty, or more calls during the night, drive out to the far west end of the city again, pick up the truck, and drive back into the same neighbourhood I was running all night in the fire truck, to deliver water. At around two-thirty in the afternoon, I would finish delivering water and hightail it back to water plant to drop off the truck, pick up the Volvo, and scoot back into the city core before I was late for my night shift. When I got back to the fire hall after a sleepless night running calls and a fire or two and then a full day slugging water bottles, I was totally exhausted to the point of feeling ill.

After another busy night shift, I was driving the water truck on August 2, 2005, when an Air France Airbus A340, during a torrential rainstorm, ran off the end of a runway at Toronto Pearson International Airport and crashed into the Etobicoke Creek. All the traffic around the airport came to a standstill with responding emergency vehicles and rubber-necked drivers drawn to the crash. After another exhausting day of delivering water and trying to return the truck to the plant I got stuck in the gridlock. It was going to take me a long time to get back to the core of the city for my night shift. Normally, I would be able to make it back to the fire hall by four in the afternoon, but this time I didn't make it back until half past six. The captain I was relieving at the time was not impressed.

The only upside to the exhaustive physical regimen my dire financial situation dictated was that the sheer volume of physical work and lack of sleep burned off any bit of body fat I had on my body. In late August of 2005, at the age of 42, I attained the best physical conditioning in my life and finally won Natural Mr. Canada after eight years of unsuccessful attempts. It seems every hardship has an upside.

After a year and a half of slugging water, my financial footing was secure enough that I could cut back on the water delivery work. I was making ends meet and finished dealing with the dispersal of assets and paying off my lawyer fees. I could recharge my physical and mental batteries.

BACK AT WORK THAT WINTER day, we answered an alarm call in a high-rise. Russ Vernon, a funny guy who twirled his hair a lot, was my crewmate. People were cluttering the lobby. We both took notice of the crowd that met us — not a good sign, for that building anyway. Normally, because alarm calls were so common here, the tenants rarely assembled in the lobby. The fact that the tenants felt they needed to evacuate their apartments alerted us to an emergency situation. Someone had pulled the alarm on the seventh floor, and the tenants told us there was smoke in the stairwells on the way down.

We made it to the seventh floor. Billy, my captain, Russ, and I made our way down the smoky hallway. A soot-smudged man was standing outside the doorway of a smoking apartment. He was so skinny he looked like a burnt matchstick wearing jockey shorts. He was also swaying back and forth, and since there wasn't a noticeable breeze in the seventh-floor hallway, we figured something was wrong.

We had dealt with this dude before. When he was drunk, he would call 911 about his asthma. There was never anything wrong with him; he just liked attention. With a pronounced slur, he filled us in on the situation. "There'sh someone inside."

The smoke was thick and black. It didn't bode well for his buddy. "Where?" I asked him.

"On the couch. I couldn't wake him up." Holy shit.

We masked up and crawled into the black smoke, Russ and I making our way by feel. There was zero visibility, but we found the couch and the man lying on it. Russ and I tried to pull him off onto the floor, but he was a very portly man. He rolled out of our grasp like a huge chunk of pizza dough, but we each managed to grab onto an arm and dragged him out into the hallway.

A second crew arrived, set up a hose line, and entered the apartment to attack the fire. In the light we could see that we were dragging an obese man of about sixty. We laid him on the floor of the hallway, grabbed a cylinder left by the second crew, and administered oxygen to the fat man.

The fire captain from the hose line crew came out of the apartment, took off his mask, and told Billy that the fire was knocked down. The kitchen was toast and smoke was venting nicely out the balcony door. Good, Billy nodded.

The skinny fire victim stood wobbly-legged over the fat man as we gave the guy oxygen. Captain Billy asked Matchstick if he'd been drinking. "Yeah," he said, then slumped over and slid down the wall into a sitting position, leaving a sooty smudge.

We told the guy he should go to the hospital, as he'd taken a lot of smoke. With the conviction of a pope, he asked, "Is one of us going to make it?"

Russ and I looked at each other. "Nope," Russ said. Matchstick closed one eye, trying to focus. "You both are."

The fat guy on the ground opened his eyes, then closed one and tried to focus as well.

Captain Billy asked Matchstick what had happened.

"I picked up my date at the bar," he said. What? On previous 911 visits he'd showed us pictures of his husband, a good-looking man. "I know how to pick 'em," he'd said.

We looked at the drunken slob on the floor mumbling to Russ. I guess Mr. Matchstick's husband was out of town. Billy asked Matchstick how the fire started, and he told us in his very drunken manner that he had been cooking bacon and eggs, minus the eggs. Blah, blah, blah.

A housefly was riding up and down on the victim's lip as he mumbled through his story. It was mesmerizing. As I watched in amazement, his voice faded out. The only sound I heard was in my mind: the pounding of the fly's little feet as it trotted across the top of the man's lip, riding it like a cowboy on a bucking bronco.

Russ and I couldn't contain ourselves. We started to giggle uncontrollably as the fly hung on for dear life. The man kept yammering, totally oblivious.

Billy told us to shut up and let buddy know that he couldn't stay in his apartment. The kitchen was gutted and there was heavy smoke damage in the rest of the place.

Focusing *avec* one eye closed, Matchstick said, "I'm going back to the bar, then. Get me my pants." He struggled to his feet and stepped over to the fat man. "Larry, come on. Let's go back to the bar."

The fat man mumbled and took off the oxygen mask. The two, arm in arm and wearing only underwear and socks, walked towards the elevator looking like Laurel and Hardy after rolling in a coal bin.

43

Torch Boy

QUEEN'S PARK, THE SITE OF Ontario's provincial legislature, is where we as a democratic society of freethinking people can voice our displeasure (in a nonviolent manner, of course) with our elected representatives. This right is non-discriminatory, meaning that any whack job can hold up a sign and say he's being screwed by the man.

Since our fire station was the closest one to Queen's Park, we forged an alliance, in concert with the police and EMS, to create a unit designed specifically for dealing with potential threats to the legislature. The unit came about because of an incident at the American consulate in the late nineties. During a daytime protest, someone threw a Molotov cocktail through a window. While I'm all for daytime cocktails, Molotovs are the kind filled with gasoline and a flaming rag that explode into a fiery ball on impact. The interior of the building was set on fire.

At the time, there was no concrete protocol in place to deal with such an incident, one that required a fire truck and crews to work their way through an angry crowd numbering in the thousands. The threat of violence was real for both the firefighters and the poor bastards inside — the consulate workers — dealing with the fire. Another complication is that a consulate, like an embassy (in this case the American one), is under foreign control. Being Canadians, we had no jurisdiction across that border.

Toronto created its Public Order Unit, affectionately known as POU (yes, that's pronounced *poo*). Whenever large crowds of people gathered at either the American consulate or the provincial legislature, our truck was assigned to the event and placed on standby. Sometimes we staged close to the gathering. Most of the time, though, the protests were peaceful — teachers wanting more prep time before class, nurses wanting less waiting time in hospitals — and we would hang out at the fire hall and monitor the situation from there. If necessary, we were dispatched via the onsite police command post.

Typically, peaceful rallies gave Station 314 a much-needed break. Our truck did as many as 4,700 emergency calls a year, so any opportunity to relax for two or three hours in a row was a bonus. But it had an impact on the run totals at the end of the year; sometimes we would miss the fifteen or twenty calls that we normally ran on a busy day because we were busy monitoring a protest.

ON ONE WINTRY DAY, WE were standing by for a farmers' protest. Tractors of all sorts surrounded Queen's Park and dumped hay in front of the legislature, to give the Big Bad City a country feel, I guess. We sat in the fire hall monitoring the radio and watching the protest unfold on TV. It looked like it would be another boring wait.

A dispatch came through to the hall — a guy was threatening to set himself on fire. I envisioned someone immolating himself on the sidewalk like the Buddhist monk who was protesting the Vietnam War. *Jeez*, I thought, *those farmers are serious guys!* Off we went to deal with another crazy situation.

As we approached, I told the crew to look sharp because there were news cameras all over the place and we didn't want to appear unprofessional (especially since I was the acting captain). As we turned onto University Avenue, at the foot of Queen's Park, we were hit by a strong smell of gasoline. Okay, this was bad.

Behind a police barricade was a white rental van with its windows covered by cardboard. The van was dodging back and forth towards the police officers who were trying to approach it, causing them to jump out of the way. Every time the van moved, we could see gasoline flowing out the rear doors.

This was seriously not good. As one newspaper article put it, "The firefighters couldn't see into the vehicle, but they could do the math: rented truck, anti-government rally, the smell of gasoline. The answer: the 1995 attack on a U.S. government building with an 1,800 kilogram fuel-and-fertilizer bomb, carried in a rented truck, that killed 168 people."

I had spoken to an unfortunate firefighter who had actually answered that call in Oklahoma City. He said the first thing he saw when he jumped off the rig was a woman's head on fire. Although the images on CNN showed tremendous damage to the structure, the firefighter said the real horror was behind the building. Men, women, and children had been blown out the back of the structure, striking the office building behind it and splattering like bugs on a car windshield.

I looked at the hundreds of spectators and news crews scrambling to get a closer look at the van. All I could think was, *When this van blows, it's going to leave a huge crater and all of us will be dead.* I shouted at a cameraman as he peeked out from behind a tree. "Get the fuck out! He's got a bomb in there!" A woman pushing a stroller was approaching the police line. *Nobody is listening. There are too many people. We're all dead!*

I guess I experienced what I can only imagine are the thoughts a soldier might have at the moment when he realizes he's not going to survive, but if he jumps on the grenade, maybe he can still save his buddies. It actually felt very calming. It brought a kind of clarity. I thought, since I was dead anyway, I had better do my best to snuff this thing out.

The man inside, whose name was Anh Ngoc Vuong, was threatening to light himself on fire. "Firemen, stay away!"

I told the guys to set up the hose lines and called dispatch to send a rescue squad, because this crazed maniac was trying to drive his van into the police cars that had him penned in. Over the next half-hour he dodged back and forth, spinning his tires and stopping just short of hitting the cruisers. At one point he took a gas can, poured it all over himself, and brandished a pair of lighters. Christ, this wingnut was going to do it. By that point we had hose lines deployed, so we waited.

"Firemen, move back!"

I advised my driver, Jeff Gayman, to back up the truck. As he backed up, we pulled off more hose so we were still in the same position to attack the fire, if and when it happened. The Emergency Task Force (ETF) advised me that they were going to break the windows in the van and would give me the heads-up when they pulled it off. (Breaking the windows is ETF protocol. It enables them to look inside for people who are likely either armed or being held hostage.) We would need to flood the van as quickly as possible to reduce the chance of an explosion and many senseless deaths.

Vuong jammed the van into reverse and backed up, forcing an officer to jump out of the way. A police cruiser sped up to meet the van and hit it head-on, smashing the front of the cruiser and van. The ETF crew ran forward to take out the windows. We rushed up to the passenger side lugging the hose to stop the man from blowing us all to bits. Vuong lit up.

Anyone who has lost their eyebrows lighting a propane barbecue after a couple of failed attempts can imagine what a barbecue the size of a panel van can do. The blast blew the truck outwards like a pop can bursting in a freezer. Flames singed my eyebrows. The inside of the van was engulfed in a fireball.

As I ran forward, I opened up the nozzle on my hose line and tried to extinguish the man. He wouldn't go out; there was just too much gasoline inside the truck. One of the crew from the rescue squad, Peter Bader, ran to the driver's door and hauled him out, still completely aflame. For expedience, I pushed the hose line through the flames in the broken passenger window for Peter to use on him instead of wasting precious seconds hauling it around the two crumpled vehicles. Then I ran around to the driver's side to help Peter with the victim.

Peter had been trying to extinguish the man by patting out the fire with his hands, but gasoline kept squishing out of Vuong's clothing and relighting. I tried to rip off his burning clothes and Peter used the hose to extinguish the flames. According to the news footage, though both of us were working feverishly to put out the fire, Vuong burned for about forty-five seconds. Blood was flowing amid the broken glass.

Once he stopped burning and was inside the ambulance, I advised Jeff to accompany the EMS crew with an extinguisher — the guy's remaining clothes and hair were still soaked with fuel filling the ambulance with volatile fumes. He was wearing two pairs of pants, two jackets, two sweaters, gloves, and a balaclava. This guy had just wanted to make a scene. He figured he was going to light himself up, burning his outer clothes only, and then let the firefighters save him, making a dramatic political statement but ultimately getting saved in the nick of time. The thing is, the extra clothing just wicked up the gasoline, making it extremely difficult to put him out once he was on fire.

The other crews on scene attacked the fire in the van while we were dealing with the man. Inside the van we found two large Rubbermaid containers full of gasoline that hadn't exploded.

Vuong, who reportedly suffered from psychiatric issues, survived and is alive today.

44

The Village

IN THE RUNNING DISTRICT OF 314 is the gay village, a neighbourhood just east of Yonge Street. The heart of the Village sits at the corner of Church and Wellesley. Toronto has the largest population of gay folks in North America, next to New York City and San Francisco. And as you may have realized already, those people know how to party!

I lived in that neighbourhood for several years, and being stationed on a truck that ran the Village, I knew I was seeing things that no redneck hetero would ever be privy to.

The inclusivity of the gay culture into contemporary society has evolved after decades of struggles by strong individuals advocating equal treatment under the law. When I came on the job in 1985, the older men I worked with were still part of the prejudiced society of the day and boasted about throwing eggs at gays during the Halloween drag parades; the predecessor of what we now know as Pride Day celebrations. During the 1950s in Toronto, gay men would ask to "meet me under the clock," in reference to the clock tower of the St. Charles Tavern on Yonge Street, a bar that served as an underground venue for men to socialize with others of their sexual orientation away from judgemental eyes. The clock tower was the original clock tower of Fire Hall #3, which was built in 1871 and closed in 1926 when the current Fire Hall #3, my fire hall, opened and later renumbered as 314.

There were several bathhouses in the Village with names such as Steamworks and Barbed Wire. These were places where you could rent a little room complete with bed, locker, and and a TV playing porn. You could also have a steam and maybe work out in the gym. I'm not sure, but I think the odd sexual encounter might have gone on in those little rooms. Maybe the monstrous bowl of condoms at the check-in desk was a clue.

Some bathhouses catered to the older, more established gentleman, some to the younger party boy, and others to the hardcore "I'm going to hurt you" kind of man. After a few years of answering medical calls to the bathhouses for drug overdoses and alcohol-related stuff, we'd find ourselves sucked in by the selection of video entertainment. After a while we'd realize, "Hey, I've seen this one. Watch this guy. Holy shit, no way is he going to ... Wow, impressive!"

Impressive is the word to describe what we experienced one night with a man who had taken a popular drug known as GHB. Once the high is gone the user crashes hard and falls into a deep sleep. This guy had obviously "fallen asleep" during the act: he was standing erect, oblivious to the half-dozen onlookers. We put his underwear on and tried to hide his goods but, impressed or not, I'm not a magician. I couldn't hide it or even stretch the underwear — it was impossible. Sure enough, when paramedics showed up to take this dude to the hospital, it was two women who answered the call.

We had to search the guy's storage drawer looking for identification, which involved rummaging through his toys to find his wallet. I got a kick out of watching the young guys who came in from other areas of the city to ride the truck. They were shell-shocked by the goings-on — innocent lambs being led to the slaughter.

One of the things about working downtown that made the job so interesting was the diversity of the calls. One minute you would be fighting a fire in an underground parking lot or forty stories above ground in a high-rise, the next you might be lifting an incubator with a one-pound preemie baby inside for an EMS crew, and the one after that you might be tending to a man who had been gang-raped at a party.

DURING A BUSY SATURDAY NIGHT, we answered a medical call to a lesbian bar, right around last call. We had to fight our way into the club through the throngs of people leaving to take cabs, seeking some privacy with new "friends." An "assertive" woman led us to a front room, where we found a butch-looking lesbian holding her head. Blood was streaming down her face. Someone had thrown a beer bottle and hit her on the noggin. My partner, Russ, and I checked out her cut; she needed a stitch or two.

As we were wiping off the blood, Captain Billy looked at the dispatch sheet. "It says here CPR is in progress. Is the ambulance here?" he asked.

"Yeah, in the back," said the assertive woman. Holy shit, this was the wrong patient! Russ and I taped a bandage to her head, grabbed our stuff, and headed over to the real emergency.

We pushed our way to the back room. Sure enough, the ambulance crew had come in the back door and were doing compressions on a patient on the stage. The performer, a twenty-five-year-old drag queen, had collapsed while singing "I Will Survive." *Thud.*

We had to take off her dress and pull out her falsies to place the defibrillator pads. Her irises were complete pinholes — probably an overdose. We assisted the paramedics by doing chest compressions and ventilations as they pumped drugs into the patient. After about forty-five minutes of chest compressions while the paramedics followed their complete protocol, injecting the entire cycle of drugs, they pronounced him dead, following directions from their base hospital. The compressions stopped. The IV lines were taken out of the patient. A sheet was pulled over the dead man's face.

As we stepped back after frantically trying to save this person's life, another drag queen came up and spoke to the paramedics. She casually told them that the man under the sheet was from Montreal and spoke only French, so she could translate when he woke up.

The man was lying on the floor under a cotton sheet — a universal sign that he wouldn't be needing a translator. Incredulous, one of the paramedics spoke to the performer — who seemed to be whacked out on drugs — as if she were a child: "He ... is ... dead."

The drag queen started wailing. "I want to cry, but the tears won't come," she said. "He has a boyfriend in Montreal. Who's going to tell him?" We tried to calm her down as she continued to scream.

The butch lesbian with the bandage on her head wandered into the back room looking for help. So now we had one dead female impersonator lying under a blanket on the floor, one very lively female impersonator screaming like crazy, jumping across the stage, and one very pissed-off butch lesbian looking to rumble.

THE TORONTO FIRE DEPARTMENT HAS been participating in Pride celebrations for several years, adding fire trucks and firefighters to the parade. Firefighters walk the parade route with Super Soaker water guns jousting with the partiers, a traditional activity, during what is typically a hot summer day. One afternoon when I was still working at Regent Park, I ended up in the Pride celebrations by accident.

On the afternoon of the parade, we responded to a report of a person trapped in an elevator on Yonge Street. The parade was wasn't to start for thirty minutes or so but people were starting to gather along the route. Once we located which floor the trapped person was on, it took a few minutes for our crew to extricate them. The captain wrote down the information of the person, and we grabbed our tools and walked out the front door of the apartment building. By now the sidewalk was packed with parade revellers and our truck had disappeared. My captain radioed the driver trying to find out where he went.

"The police told me to move the truck. I'm up on College Street around the corner," said the driver. College Street was the next block north but the parade had now started and the sidewalks were chock a block full of people. Dressed in our fire gear, we pressed our way through the crowd to try to locate our missing truck. Many people thought we were just partiers enjoying the parade. We encountered several men in fire gear from different cities celebrating Pride and I was cruised a few times, just like I was when I lived in the neighbourhood years before.

One year a couple of firefighter friends of mine from the College Street Fire Hall, #315, participated in Pride celebrations. Both are gay and were dressed in their Toronto Fire gear. A photographer from the *Toronto Sun* snapped a photo of them celebrating Pride Day with a kiss. The photo made the front page of the paper. The two men got much light-hearted ribbing and the photo was framed and placed on the wall of 315 alongside photos of significant fires and rescues — a hall of fame, of sorts. Years later, however, there was a reminder that, although Pride is a sanctioned event embraced by most firefighters, not all were on board. A fire chief of significant rank walked into 315 and saw the photo on the wall of fame. He demanded the acting captain take down the "revolting photograph." The acting captain did as he was told. News travelled across the job. The crew were pissed off and responded in protest. The photograph was replaced with a picture of Margaret Atwood, a vision of culture and inclusion. It still hangs on the wall to remind the crew at 315 that bigots are still out there. The crews complained about the action of the chief and he was disciplined, and ordered to take sensitivity training. Part of his punishment was handing out fire recruitment flyers at the corner of Church and Wellesley.

45

Injured Inside and Out

MOST FIREFIGHTERS SUFFER SOME SORT of injury in their career. The majority are cuts and sprains from the physical nature of the work: bad backs, bad knees. One of the most serious injuries I suffered during my thirty-two-year career — aside from the whole mental breakdown thing — was a torn biceps.

Technically it didn't happen on department time, but it was during a fire department activity: old-timers' hockey. Actually, it wasn't even during the game; it was after I got home. I had gotten stuck in traffic on the way back to my place and had to take a pee in the worst way. When I got home, I was in such a hurry that I tripped going down the stairs, ripping my biceps trying to stop myself from being killed by the fall.

So there I was, lying at the bottom of my basement stairs with a torn arm. My biceps muscle had ripped away from the elbow and was curled up in my armpit. It would need surgery for sure. But more importantly right then, I had to urinate before I exploded. So imagine me there in my basement washroom, unzipping my jeans with my good arm, pissed off at myself for tearing my biceps, and doing my best not to piss on myself.

I drove to the hospital in my little MINI Cooper, shifting with my good arm and steering with my knee while clutching at the same time, a balancing act the likes of which hadn't been seen since the Chinese acrobats appeared on the *Ed Sullivan Show*. I got to the hospital and drove my MINI into the hospital lot. I became very pissed off again — the parking was going to cost me twenty dollars! Unfortunately, universal health care doesn't cover parking.

Just after surgery and somewhere in my drug-induced haze, I recall the doctor telling me everything would be all right. I'd have to do rehab for several weeks. For me, rehab consisted of shovelling snow from the driveway with my good arm and drinking at the pub. After six weeks of rehab, my liver needed to get back to work. I would just have to ease into it.

AFTER BEING BACK AT WORK for three minutes, I faced the biggest fire of my career.

In the early hours of a February morning, a fire broke out in a block of buildings built in the 1880s — stores with apartments above them. It started in an electronics shop and had gone undetected for a while, allowing it to get a foothold in the historic buildings. By the time we arrived for work that morning, the night crew had already been fighting this rapidly moving fire for a couple of hours. We'd have to relieve the crew at the fire and take over operations so those boys and girls could go home and get a well-deserved rest.

The fire department's available resources were strained at that point and there was no one available to shuttle relief crews to the fire. Plan B: call the police and ask for a cruiser to drive the team to the gig. Unfortunately the fire had now spread to seven buildings and the entire downtown core was a traffic mess. Every available cop was busy diverting traffic away from the burning buildings. Enough of waiting around for the logistics to work themselves out. Those guys needed to be relieved. So just like the Clampetts on *The Beverly Hillbillies*, we all jumped into one of the crew's pickup truck and ran ourselves down to the fire.

We found our guys at the front edge of the fire and arranged to change over our equipment, including masks, radios, and lights. The crew was set up with a water monitor (a high-volume hose nozzle) on the street in front of the last burning building in the row, trying to halt the forward progress of the fire. My counterpart was inside the building next door, looking for signs that the fire had extended into that structure.

There was a loud creak and a ball of fire shot up over our heads then the entire five-storey building collapsed in front of us with a rumble like a freight train. We dodged flying timber and bricks as a firefighter in front of me jumped on his crewmate to shelter him from the falling walls.

My first instinct was to rush forward into the crash. My friend was inside the structure that the building had fallen into. A few times in my career when a building collapsed, my first thought was to rush forward to see if my friends had been hurt. In this instance I got to the front door of the building next to the collapse. My friend, the captain I was relieving, was climbing out over the smouldering timbers.

"So, what's new?" I asked him.

"Not much. Quiet night."

It was macho swagger on the outside, but inside we were both a mess, and tremendously relieved that no one had been killed or seriously hurt.

IN THE CORE OF TORONTO, there's an energy company that uses steam to heat buildings. A grid system of pipes connects the downtown office towers to several steam generation plants strategically placed to cover as many buildings as possible. We answered a call to one of its steam-generating plants, where two men had been caught inside a large containment tank during a possible chemical flash fire. Imagine lighting a hibachi after pouring a can of barbecue starter on the briquettes — you get the picture. This was a confined-space rescue, which required a specialized crew and equipment. We on Pumper 314 were to be the medical team, assisting one of the rescue squads dispatched to perform the technical rescue.

When we arrived, a worker outside told us to relax; the guys were out of the tank. Inside the plant we were led to the stairs to make our way to the second floor to tend to the men.

On the first landing we found a man with melted skin hanging from his hands. I radioed to the incoming crew to bring extra burn kits — this was more than just a couple of guys who had fallen into a big tank. The man swore a few times, then told me his son was still upstairs, where they had been working. The father-and-son team had been contracted to clean the inside of a steam-storage tank fifteen feet high and about five feet in diameter. They had been using chemical cleaners to scrub the interior of the tank when something went wrong.

The squad crew showed up with a burn kit, so I left the man with them and followed my partner, Russ, upstairs into the plant. The smell of chemical cleaners and paint was overwhelming. Had we entered an explosive environment? There had been mention of a flash fire in the dispatch ...

We found the man's son lying on the ground. He was about twenty-five years old, but he looked like a rookie makeup artist had tried to make him look a hundred. It was as if a grey mask had been draped over the young man's face: a mask made of someone else's skin.

As we started cutting off the man's clothes, he mumbled to us, pleading for painkillers. His body was soaked, but his hair wasn't singed and his clothes weren't burned. The fire marshal's investigator later told me that flash fires always give off moisture. Still, this guy was drenched.

The poor guy was in pain, and we did our best to cut off his clothes without pulling off his skin with them. It occurred to me that he wasn't actually burned. He had been steamed — like a lobster.

His whole body was pruned up, like the bottom of your feet after you sit in the tub for too long. The grey mask had been his face, and now it was sliding off. Even his tongue was degloving, stripping off like the skin of a grape; he was spitting out bits of flesh while we worked on him.

When the father-and-son team went in to work on the tank, a series of lockouts had been put in place. Valves were turned off and locked to bypass that section of the plant in order to stop steam from entering the storage tank while they were inside. Unfortunately for them, an emergency relief valve somewhere down the line opened to vent an over-pressurized tank, and the live steam had found its way into the tank the son was inside. Without warning, he was boiled like a hot dog. Upon hearing the screams, the father reached down into the tank and pulled up his son.

The father died first; the live steam he had breathed in had scalded the inside of his lungs. The son died later that night. An inquest resulted in the company being fined the largest amount ever in the province's history for safety infractions resulting in a work-related death. The story stays with me; the image of the young man looking up at me pleading for painkillers haunts me still.

Running nonstop and sheer diversity of calls on the busy fire truck had kept my mind off of disturbing memories that were starting to clutter up my head. No time to dwell on old tragedies. But soon I started facing serious situations on the job with a cavalier attitude. Maybe it was the beginning of me subconsciously trying to preserve my increasingly fragile sanity. I was getting a taste of burnout.

46

A Promotion to Captain

I FINALLY GOT PROMOTED TO the rank of captain in February 2010. My new fire hall, #344, was built in 1910 and originally housed horses and a steam engine. It was also used as the Toronto Fire Department training facility until 1980. Photos of previous classes line the walls of the sitting room.

Station 344 is in the Annex, a section of the city close to the University of Toronto, just outside the downtown core. My new truck, Pumper 344, didn't do 4,700 calls a year like Pumper 314, but rather a more humane 2,800: somewhat fewer false alarms and a lot more fires. I had moved on from rooming houses to fraternity houses. My drunk quota changed as well ... sort of.

I left a district of down-and-out drunks for a district of university drunks, which was not necessarily any better. At least with the older drunks I could understand what the hell they were saying. It seems like when kids say something is bad it's really good. "That's sick! You guys are the shit!" Those are good things, apparently.

However, "I'm sick with the shits," does not mean you are cool in either lingo. One time during frosh week we had a first-year, first-time drunk student who had passed out from too much alcohol. She looked cool in her leather jacket and fishnet stockings, that is, until she crapped herself and the poo pushed out through her fishnets, creating a pile of mushy french-fry turds.

I embraced my new role as captain. As an acting captain for many years I was confident in my abilities on the fire ground, but as an acting captain I was sort of the hired hand only in charge of my truck when my captain was off duty or being shipped to any truck that needed a captain for the day. I wanted my own crew. I wanted a home to finish out my career. I had worked at 344 in the past and I was thankful to be posted to such a storied fire hall with a great history and a great running area. My new crew at 344 had been working together for a few years and I knew most of them from years of running fires where the running districts of 314 and 344 intersected.

Every fire department, every district, and even every apparatus has their own way of doing things based on the firefighting style of the crew and the geographical or socioeconomic makeup of their particular running area. For example, a pumper crew working in a suburban neighbourhood will require a different hose layout than a crew working in a dense urban area of the city. The suburban crew had wide streets and long front lawns while the urban crew dealt with narrow streets and would have to access the back of a row of houses via a rear laneway. Luckily for me, my new crew was a well-seasoned group that welcomed me into their world and filled me in on the unique attributes of my new running district.

One of the first non-fire calls at my new digs was for a report of a young man who had fallen in the yard of a fraternity house. It was a bitterly cold night as we got off the truck in front of a fraternity house that we responded to frequently for students that had overdrank and needed help. At the time I was preoccupied, as I had just had a spat with one of my sons. It was a dumb argument, but my son was upset with me and wouldn't talk to me. I was angry with myself for hurting his feelings.

We were ushered to the back of the large frat house to the parking lot. A young man, twenty-one years old, lay crumpled on the pavement. One of my crew slipped and fell on his frozen blood as he approached to assess the boy. My job as the captain of a medical response is to gather as much information as possible about the victim — name, age, etc. — and the circumstances of the accident. Upon investigation it was revealed that the boy had locked himself outside on the fire escape during a party and attempted to crawl into an open window, slipping on the icy roof and falling, hitting the fire escape, on the way down.

I looked at the boy. He was dead. Head smashed. Fingers mangled from when he had bounced off the fire escape before he hit the pavement. My crew and the incoming paramedics worked frantically to save this young man. In my mind I saw what could have been one of my sons, now the same age as the dead boy. Same size, same hair colour, same style of clothing. I flashed back to how depressed and hurt I felt when I couldn't see my boys after I first left Linda and had to fight to see them. I hurt for the parents of this young man. I could imagine and could feel what they would feel upon learning their boy, his whole exciting life ahead of him, had died in an accident.

Another memorable call, six months later, that affected me by resurfacing dormant depressive thoughts was for a man collapsed in a backyard of an apartment house.

Our truck arrived, and as we jumped off, we were directed by tenants who lived upstairs in the large house. We were told that they were having a party the night before and saw the old man who lived in the basement drinking on a lounger in the backyard. He was in the same position this morning and thought someone should check on him. *Hey, why didn't you check on him, neighbour?*

We walked down the driveway to the backyard where we found the man lying on a lounger just like the tenant said. From a distance it appeared this man, in his sixties, had passed out drunk. A large empty bottle of Jack Daniels whiskey stood next to the lounger.

A bust of Elvis Presley sat on the lawn next to him. As we approached we realized this man was not just passed out drunk. Blood was dripping down from his throat and from his forearms. Bees were buzzing all around him; some were crawling out from large cuts to his neck and the crux of his elbows. A box cutter knife was on the grass next to him. The man had been dead for many hours. It's too bad the partiers didn't bother to check on him earlier.

He was pronounced dead by the attending paramedics via the base hospital we work under and the coroners arrived a short time later to take the body to the morgue. It was the morning of August 17, the day after the anniversary of Elvis Presley's death. It appears the man was mourning the loss of his hero and took his own life. It was another reminder to me that suicide is so final. I was glad I didn't have the heart to do it.

But the problem now remained how to place the bee-covered corpse into the body bag to be transported to the morgue.

With the dignity of the man being our priority, we did our best to shoo off the bees and bandage up the cuts to stop the bees from further feeding on the blood sugar. Since the coroner's team had no protective clothing, our crew covered up with bunker gear and gloves to pick up the body, place it in the body bag, and carry it away from the swarm of bees. The body bag was placed into the hearse and we went back to the lounger to wash off the blood with water and bleach for the sake of the tenants. Another lonely soul had taken his life. Over the years I've seen dozens of suicides and each one makes me look within myself. I'm so thankful to now be on the other side of my own suicidal thoughts.

47

The Assailant Is in the Building

TO GET ON THE FIRE department now, young hopefuls first have to do a pre-fire course at a community college. One of the guys on my truck had a neighbour who was a cop and who asked him if his daughter could do a ride-along for her college course. Cool, no problem, although she'd have to pay the standard fee in the standard currency: we preferred muffins to doughnuts.

The young woman arrived with a whack-load of muffins and won us over immediately when her dad showed us his gun. After hugs and kisses, Officer Dad left his daughter to hang out at the fire hall and ride the truck for the day.

It seems that whenever we had someone ride along on the trucks, it always ended up being a slow, boring day. I have no idea why; I'm not up on the whole karma thing. With that in mind, I explained to this young lady that she was probably facing a day full of nothing.

Ten minutes later we got a call for alarms ringing. I explained to her that she would get a taste of what it's like to answer a false alarm. "You'll get a lot of those." A radio update while we were en route said there was smoke in the place, a rooming house.

We arrived and found people standing on the sidewalk in front of the house. Okay, maybe this wasn't a false alarm, which was good for our ride-along. I turned to her and told her that the activity in front of the address is a signal that something could be happening inside. I told her to stick close to the truck when I went in to investigate. She nodded. She seemed to be enjoying the experience.

Once I exited the truck, a tenant of the building pointed the way and said there was a fire in the kitchen and other tenants were trapped in the basement; smoke was coming from a basement window. I called in to dispatch to send a working-fire response: basically a squad and a support vehicle to add to the normal first-alarm response of two pumpers, an aerial ladder truck, and a district chief.

We dragged in a hose line and headed for the basement. The stairs were on fire, so we had to fight our way down them to search for the trapped tenants. The smoke was thick; we prodded around on hands and knees looking for people. There were several doors downstairs and it would take a bit of time to search the rooms behind them. We opened one door and could see light from a window through the smoke, probably the same window I had seen smoke coming out of when we arrived. The three of us — my two crew members and I — groped around, looking for someone, anyone.

As the smoke vented out the window and cleared a bit, we could see that we were in an apartment. On the radio we heard that another crew had rescued a female tenant with severe burns. The captain was asking for a rush on an ambulance to the rear of the building. Then he said that the victim's throat had been slashed and they wanted the police to the back ASAP.

A second victim was pulled from the building by crews working another part of the fire. As we tackled the basement fire, the other crews were rescuing trapped tenants. The smoke cleared a bit more and we saw that the wall and the back of the door were smeared with blood — lots and lots of blood.

An emergency tone came over the radio: "Attention all crews, attention all crews. The assailant is still in the building." Not a message you want to hear when you're standing inside a burning building sloshing around in the victim's blood.

It was around this time that the low-air alarms on our breathing apparatus started ringing. Time to get the hell out of there. Our crew exited and I took them around to the back of the building to see if we could help the crews working on the burn/slashing victim. Her body was severely burned and her clothes had been cut off. As she was rolled over onto her back, she said, "My neck hurts." Holy shit, she was still alive!

The assailant had been the woman's estranged (emphasis on *strange*) boyfriend, who lived in the same building. She was a student; he was a messed-up man. Eventually he was found inside, unconscious, and transported to hospital. She died in the ambulance. He didn't.

In addition to the butcher shop we encountered in the basement, a pool of blood was found in the kitchen on the main floor. It appeared to me that the guy slit her throat in the kitchen, dragged her downstairs to his apartment, barricaded the door, and set the stairs on fire to trap her, then went in the kitchen to commit suicide by stabbing himself. Either that or there was a third party involved who found them together, stabbed him, sliced her throat, and dumped her in the boyfriend's apartment before setting the stairs on fire to trap both of them. The police said we might never know what really happened. She was dead and he was in a coma, and chances were he wasn't going to wake up again.

I told our young ride-along that over the course of her firefighting career she may never see such a multifaceted fire with an arson, multiple trapped victims, and murder-suicide. So much for the boring day for our ride-along.

48

A Fortunate Encounter

A SHIFT OR TWO LATER we were dispatched to a report of a smouldering flower box. Not the most exciting kind of call but one we would respond to nonetheless. The building, a two-storey former corner store, was now set up as offices and as we arrived we were met by two women who worked inside.

A large flower box full of peat was smouldering, all right. It appeared, judging by the burnt wood of the flower box, it had been smouldering all night and the side of the wooden building was burning as well. We began to shovel out the dirt to hose down the burning wood when one of the women handed us a shovel she had brought from inside the office. It was a brand new lime green and chrome gardener's shovel. I commented that it was the coolest looking shovel I had ever seen and why the heck did you have one in the office? She said it was used as a prop in a television show they produced. *Oh, really? This is a television production office?*

As my crew worked on the smouldering flower box I told the two women I would need to see the inside of the building, you know, to look for fire extension and stuff. A couple of seconds later my crew came to tell me the fire was out and we were good to go. But as far as I was concerned, we weren't quite done yet. Never being one to ever let an opportunity pass to advance my screenwriting/movie-producing agenda, I elbowed my way into the office. The two women, Wendi-Jane Hayden and Adrianna Crifo, had both worked in the television/movie world for years. I unabashedly pitched myself to them and they agreed to grab a beer with me to discuss if they could help me move my writing projects forward.

We met a week later at a neighbourhood pub and sat outside on the patio. We immediately hit it off and chatted about what productions they worked on in their office and they asked what I would like to see happen with my screenplays. Over the course of the next few months we met to catch up and have beers several times.

BY THE SUMMER OF 2010, Justin and Michael had grown into confident young men. Both were in post secondary school and the cost of carrying half of the university/college tuition and rent, on top of child support, plus my own rent, was becoming onerous. I don't begrudge child support or paying for my boys' education. I'm just saying it was a slog. Money was very tight.

I dated again a couple of times that year but I found it was too much like work. I didn't enjoy myself. I felt each woman I went out with was judging me, like I was having a job interview. Since money was so tight and I couldn't buy the right clothes or afford the good restaurants, I found the whole process humiliating and exhausting. This serial monogamist was going to stay single for a while.

But then Wendi-Jane had texted me saying that she had the perfect woman for me. I told her that I was going to hold off on the dating for a bit. She said this woman was really smart and fun. She was her boyfriend's ex-wife. My first instinct was "No thanks," but I told Wendi-Jane I'd check out her profile on Facebook and let her know if I'd be interested in the future. A few months later I did eventually check out her profile and liked what I saw. I told Wendi-Jane that I would meet her single friend.

A week later the date was set for me to meet Sue, Wendi-Jane's boyfriend's ex-wife, for a coffee. Coffee would be a good first meeting because I was living in the red and didn't have any extra cash for things like a dinner in a restaurant. The day before the coffee date, I woke to find my dog, a Tibetan terrier named Tsampa, lying sick in her bed. Her one eye completely swollen shut as if Mike Tyson had punched her. I picked her up and took her down the block to the vet. After an examination the doctor told me Tsampa had an infected tooth that had caused her eye to swell. It would cost about $700 to have the vet put Tsampa under general anaesthetic, remove the tooth, and drain the infection. Sure Doc, let's do it. Although it was money that I could ill afford, I just ventured a little deeper into the overdraft of my chequing account. *Upward towards zero!* was my battle cry during my many lean years. From the vet's office I texted Wendi-Jane that I wouldn't be able to meet Sue, with the perpetually lame excuse that my dog was sick.

49

Dreams Do Come True

IN DECEMBER OF THAT YEAR, I eventually did, by chance, meet Sue. Wendi-Jane texted me that she was at the Balmy Beach Club having pre-Christmas drinks. I always wanted to be, and eventually did become, a member of the BBC, a canoe and social club that dates back to 1905 and has spawned many Olympic athletes over the last century. The Balmy Beach Club has the best patio in the city, overlooking the lake that I've used to watch Canada Day fireworks or to just enjoy a beer in the sun and watch the beach volleyballers. Wendi-Jane was with her boyfriend Cameron Carpenter — a man who lived in the rock world I've always dreamed about. He'd worked with artists like Stevie Wonder and Slash from Guns 'n' Roses, and had discovered bands like Sloan and the Headstones. Sue was at the club as well.

Wendi-Jane introduced me to Sue, a tall, beautiful blonde. In my semi-drunken state, she seemed about a foot taller than me.

"Hi," I said. "You've got a good nose." WTF? *What just came out of my mouth?* Well, I blew that, I thought. I wandered off to talk to someone else to reduce my chance of embarrassing myself further.

Sue's son Kyle had just come in from McGill University, home for Christmas to meet his parents at the BBC for a Christmas drink. I chatted with Kyle for a while, totally impressed with him. A really nice guy: smart, and a writer too. Kyle would later play drums with me and my band at my fiftieth birthday bash a few years later.

After the bar at the Balmy Beach Club closed down, Wendi-Jane, Cameron, Sue, and I trudged down the road through the snow to a bar to watch some live music. Sue, a self-proclaimed music head — having lived for years with Cameron hanging with artists like the Ramones, Lenny Kravitz, the Backstreet Boys, and Britney Spears — loved live music. Years earlier Sue and Cam even helped an ambitious young singer-songwriter make a few extra dollars by having her babysit for them: Alanis Morissette.

The four of us had a great time — Cam, his girlfriend, his ex-wife, and me. The arrangement sounds peculiar, but Sue and Cam are still good friends and it works well for all involved.

Still reluctant to get into a serious relationship, Sue and I kept it casual. Neither of us was interested in any more drama in our lives. I kept my distance emotionally, knowing that once Sue saw me on a down cycle she might not want to deal with a person struggling mentally. I can't blame her. It's not easy at times. But after a few months we both realized we lived life at the same speed and shared the same values.

Our kids met each other at a holiday dinner and, all being within a couple of years difference in age, got along well. Kyle and Kari (Sue's daughter), Justin, and Michael celebrated with Sue and I on a beach in Aruba when we married on October 15, 2014.

Sue had never lived with a shift worker. She didn't like the long twenty-four hour shifts Toronto Fire eventually adopted, feeling lonely at night; just her and my dog Tsampa. But she was supportive and understanding when I told her I needed to be a firefighter, on a fire truck. There was no way I was going to work straight days in a fire department support division. Through much talk and patience she began to understand the frequently tormented man she loved and came to anticipate the cycles of ups and downs I experience. Sue recalls the rhythm of the schedule. Especially the last two years of my career when burnout had set in. Each tour of duty for me was a three-day ordeal for Sue. The day before my shift Sue would see my anxiety rise in anticipation of having to handle another death or traumatic event. Then during the twenty-four-hour shift of dealing with emergency situations, Sue would wonder if I was going to get hurt or if I would have to face a horrific incident that would traumatize me. Then Sue had to deal with me the day after a shift: having to sleep much of the next day. When I was on duty my time was dictated by the fires, medical and alarm calls, training schedules, and incident reports. The day after working a twenty-four-hour shift I felt I needed to have control over my day. I refused to be run by someone else's schedule, which meant I wasn't getting any jobs done around the house.

50

The Prime Minister

DURING ONE PRIDE WEEKEND WHILE working downtown, our truck answered a call for a man who had jumped from the balcony of a luxury condominium. We had just left the Yorkville Fire Hall after dropping off some paperwork and were tagged as the closest unit to the call. We arrived on scene a minute later. The victim was already on the ground. A paramedic, who happened to be in the lobby for another call, had been alerted by the building security about the jumper. He got to the man before us and placed a blanket over his body before we arrived. I was glad to see that. I didn't need another gory image to crowd my mind as I slept.

A woman on my crew, Jordan Muszynski, who was off duty that day, saw our truck at the call and stopped by. We said hello and I filled her in on the suicide jumper. She was glad not to see it as well. Jordan asked if I was free the next day. I told her yes, what's up? "Do you want to meet the Prime Minister?" Absolutely!

Prime Minister Justin Trudeau was to attend the Pride parade the next day. The Prime Minister's security team and Toronto fire-fighter staff arranged a covert photo op. When I got home the next

morning I told Sue about the photo and I asked if she wanted to
come as well. She immediately agreed.

All the firefighters meeting the PM were to congregate at my
old fire hall, #314, which is ground zero for firefighters' Pride celebrations, and a van would take us over to the arranged spot. More
firefighters than expected showed up and a few of us had to walk
the one block to where the photo was being taken. We went to
the intersection that they told us to go to, but there was no fire
truck in sight. The four of us in bunker pants walked across Carlton
Street looking for the elusive fire truck and other firefighters. A tall
man in a loud Hawaiian shirt, standing on the corner by himself,
winked at me and said, "Your guys are up the alley." He was part
of the PM's security team. We were led to an alley just off the Church
Street Village where a fire truck had been parked and waited for
Justin Trudeau.

The Prime Minister arrived with his security team a few minutes later. He came and shook everyone's hands and posed for
selfies with firefighters. One of the firefighters from #314 handed
the PM a #314 Pride T-shirt. He quickly took off his shirt and stood
bare-chested in the street as he unfolded the T-shirt to put it on.
There were a few yelps. I've got to be honest with you — I thought
Sue was going to faint when she saw his abs. The PM was fantastic
and took photos with everyone who wanted one. He even took
a selfie with the group of us in the background for the firefighter
union.

Prime Minister Justin Trudeau would walk in the Pride parade
that afternoon. It reminded me how far Pride has come from the
relatively small block party of a few thousand people that I experienced in 1985 to the million people who celebrate it every year in
Toronto.

51

Enough Is Enough

FIREFIGHTERS ANSWER MEDICAL CALLS FOR suicides and attempted suicides. They're never a pleasant experience, but thankfully I'd hit bottom often enough to understand how life can get overwhelming and the future can seem hopeless. Empathy (what little I had left of it) could go a long way. I guess that's what the Big Guy had in store for me when my life went for shit more than once.

At about five o'clock in the morning one fall day, we answered a call for a possible suicide jumper at a downtown hotel. A TV news cameraman had been driving by when he noticed a leg sticking out from the roof over the hotel's entranceway. Once inside the hotel, we went a few floors up and from there we could see out over the entrance, and there lay the crumpled body of a man. We made our way to the entranceway roof to check out the jumper. He was a young guy, about twenty-five years old, and obviously dead. We laid a sheet over him while we waited for the coroner.

By this time hotel security had figured out which room he had jumped from. We went to the room to check it out with the police to see if it was a crime scene. Was it a suicide or was he pushed?

Was he trying to escape from an assailant and jumped? Were there other victims upstairs?

There were no other victims. The young man had checked in by himself the night before. He had no luggage. It was clear that he had gone there just to end his life, away from the scrutiny of familiar eyes. We went up to the room to get an ID for the report and found his suicide note. The officer in charge passed it around for us to see. *I'm sorry Mom and Dad. I owe my roommate $5. Please pay him.*

It hit me in the gut. What could have troubled this young man so much that he felt he needed to end it all? Did he suffer from depression, like me? Was he not as fortunate as I had been to discover that your mind plays tricks on you during those times? Did he not have the blessing of wonderful friends like mine, who stepped in to help when I couldn't help myself? I have been blessed in so many ways. I don't know why. Someone was looking out for me. Someone needed me to stick around.

Affluent neighbourhoods are not immune to life's miseries. We answered a call in one such neighbourhood for an attempted suicide at a multimillion-dollar home. The police had arrived before us and were trying to get inside the house. A woman was on the second floor, shouting down to us. She said she was restraining her son, and if she let go of his arms he would shoot himself again.

The young man, only nineteen, was in the care of his mother. He had been released from a mental health facility for the weekend. He was suffering from depression but his medication wasn't helping. He had tried to kill himself. There were no guns in the house save for a pellet gun he had gotten as a young teen.

Seventeen times. Seventeen times he had taken the pellet gun, pressed it against his skin, and pulled the trigger, trying desperately to get rid of the pain. His mother, frantically holding her son's arms to stop him from hurting himself further, was eventually able to grab the gun from him. She threw the keys out the window so we could get into the home.

The young man sat in a second-floor room filled with hundreds of leather-bound books. Blood was flowing down his bare chest in neat rows where the pellets had penetrated the skin. He had shot himself several times in the head. We were able to pick some of the pellets off his skin like raisins from the top of a muffin.

The mother was frantic. I had taken her to a back room to get away from the crew working on her son. What could I say to this woman to assure her that things would be all right? Then it struck me. I could tell her that I had lived through those same dark, hopeless feelings. I could tell her with complete certainty that yes, you could come out of that shit storm intact.

When something terrible happens to people, they often ask themselves, "Why me?" I now understood why I had suffered through the things I experienced. I had suffered so I could give some hope to a distraught mother. I could look her in the eye and say, "This is not forever." I could tell a young student that I understood the scary feelings and the panic attacks. I could tell them I understood that sometimes you just need another human being there to assure you that you can weather the storm.

"Why me?" I'm glad it's me. I'm glad a thousand times. It's been a great gift.

52

The Last Big One

ONCE I'D FINALLY DECIDED TO retire and picked the actual date — February 28, 2017 — I emptied my locker at work over a period of a few weeks and moved out junk I hadn't used in years, like my boxing gloves. I hadn't punched a bag in twenty years. The foam padding in the glove turned to dust in my hand. If I actually hit some dude in the yapper while wearing them, his teeth would have flown out of his mouth because my knuckles would have broken through the glove.

Thirty-two years is a long time to dedicate to one career. I'd had highs and lows, but I was hoping I would be able to end my firefighting life with a bang instead of a whimper. I wanted a good burner that everybody would see on the news so I could say, "I was at that one!"

On my third-last shift, we were dispatched to a fire call at a racquetball club. En route we received updates on the truck's computer: the caretaker of the club had found smoke coming from a receptacle on the second floor and had put out the electrical fire with an extinguisher.

The first-arriving crew (we were the third due) would investigate and report back the status of our electrical fire. Cool. I was betting on a nothing kind of call and I made that declaration to my crew. I'd seen that kind of stuff before. No biggie.

The first-crew captain radioed to dispatch, saying there were no outward signs of smoke. They had indeed liaised with the caretaker and would investigate further. See? No biggie. A minute later, the captain indicated that there was light smoke on the second floor. Okay, it was a something call, but still no biggie.

The building was situated down an alley behind a row of restaurants and office buildings. It had originally been constructed as a streetcar barn in the early 1900s. Streetcars no longer used the facility, so it had been closed several decades before. Since then, the building had become surrounded by a wall of stores, restaurants, condominiums, and office towers as a result of development in the area. The streetcar barn had been renovated, expanded, and was now a posh racquetball club and athletic centre.

We arrived and jumped off the truck. Smoke was now pushing out the top of the building. It was no little electrical fire; this baby was rolling! I updated dispatch about the smoke coming through the roof. Okay, I sucked a bit at the prediction thing, but I was giddy at the prospect of it being a biggie. The game was on!

Our crew made its way to the front door. The initial truck, Pumper 311, was hooked up to the standpipe connection, and the pumper operator, "Ducky," directed our crew where to go in the building.

At the top of a grand set of stairs inside, the crews from Pumper 311 and Rescue 134 were hooking up to the interior standpipe (hose cabinet) and advancing a line to a mechanical room above the second-floor auditorium. When our crew entered the auditorium, it was filled with light smoke. We helped set up the attack hose line and grabbed a backup line to protect the initial crews.

The smoke quickly got thicker as my crew, Pumper 344, dragged hose up a set of narrow metal stairs to the mechanical room on the third floor. Halfway up the stairs, the heavy smoke blacked out our vision.

P311 and R134 were in the mechanical room playing water, to no effect. I could hear shouting and, a short time later, the low-air alarms on the firefighters' masks. The initial crews would have to evacuate soon, before their air ran out. The P311 crew soon exited the mechanical room. P344, my crew on the stairs backing them up, had to move down to the landing so P311 could get to the second floor and then out for fresh air cylinders.

My crew ascended the stairs again and was now backing up R134. Visibility was zero. The air was filled with the sounds of firefighters banging on the roof and the crashing of materials inside the mechanical room. My nozzle man, Robin Earl, yelled that, just a couple of steps up from where we were crouched, the heat was extreme. The guys inside the mechanical room must have been taking a beating.

I was the captain on the backup line and I couldn't see a thing. I couldn't tell if the crew inside the mechanical room was hitting fire or just blasting water into the heat. I yelled through my mask to the captain of R134, "What's going on in there? Are you hitting it?" No answer. Just the sounds of banging and shouting between the crew members inside.

I pulled up more hose to get in deeper towards the fire. My flash hood, a fire-resistant thermal-barrier balaclava, hooked on something hanging off the wall, pulling it back and exposing the side of my face to the heat. A flash of pain pierced my jawline. This was one hot fire!

I was carrying a thermal imaging camera (TIC) — Toronto Fire had placed one on every truck — strapped to my mask as I directed Robin where to spray the water. The visibility was still zero and no flames could be seen. Robin used the TIC like the screen of a video game, focusing on hitting the hot spots. (Thank you, Toronto City Council, for approving this essential and life-saving piece of equipment. TIC technology, which was developed in 1947 and provided to Toronto firefighters only seventy years later, enables the firefighter to see through smoke and allows meaningful visual readings beyond 2,000 degrees Fahrenheit. It's like night and day to be able to see through the smoke instead of probing around on your hands and knees searching for a deep-seated fire.)

"It's too hot! Back out! We gotta back out!" The mechanical room was fully involved. With the extreme heat, getting close enough to the fire to extinguish the blaze was becoming impossible.

At that point came a radio announcement from the captain of one of the crews on the floor below us. The ceiling of the second floor — the ceiling below our feet — had collapsed into the auditorium, exposing a large mass of fire. Time for us on the third floor to get the hell out before we also ended up in a pile in the second-floor auditorium. We retreated down the stairs and, protected by another hose team, out through the now fully involved auditorium.

Once clear of the fire room on the second-floor landing I used the TIC to check the ceiling temperatures outside the auditorium and down the hall. The pot lights were pushing smoke. When I pointed the camera at them, the entire ceiling flashed in the red zone of the temperature range. The fire had gotten past the interior crews and extending back through the rest of the building.

I updated the incident commander, reporting that fire was running across the ceiling of the second floor. Another collapse of the structure in the auditorium, and a firefighter rolled out onto the second-floor landing, shouting, "I can't find my captain! He was right behind me!" A mayday went out about the missing captain. Thirty seconds later he was found and led out to get medical attention, dazed and covered in debris. The call was made to go defensive, to pull out all interior crews and fight the fire from the exterior.

Outside, we met up with the initial crew at the air-refill truck. Their nozzle man was pressing snow onto the blisters on his wrists. He had developed second-degree burns as a result of trying to extinguish the fire in the mechanical room. We grabbed some Gatorade, exchanged the air cylinders on our masks for full ones, and went back to stage in front of the building, waiting for reassignment.

At this point about a dozen trucks were committed to putting out the fire.

Fire crews had commandeered the standpipe system of the condo high-rise to the rear of the racquetball club and were spraying water from several balconies on to the burning building a short six feet away. Three ladder pipes were set up, extending over adjacent storefronts, blasting water into the flames that danced across the roof of the building. An emergency tone blared over the radio. "Attention all crews! Attention all crews! Roof is compromised! Roof collapse on the south end of the building!"

At that moment an elderly lady, who had somehow circumvented the entire battalion of firefighters, walked gently over the bulging hoses and past the dozen fire trucks. She was next to one of the aerial towers that were pounding water into the raging fire before she was finally caught by an incredulous firefighter and escorted back to safety. Apparently it was membership dues day, and by God, fire or no fire, she was not going to pay a late fee! Seriously, I'm not making this up.

About six hours into the incident, we were relieved by fresh crews. P344 returned to the fire hall to clean up the equipment and grab a hot shower and a bite to eat before putting the rig back into service to run calls. After changing into fresh fatigues, I started typing up my report and lay down for a bit. I was exhausted from the fire, but quite pleased with myself. Yes, I had indeed gone out with a bang. Ultimately, the damage from the blaze was reported to be in excess of ten million dollars.

53

My Final Day on the Job

TWO SHIFTS LATER I ARRIVED at Station 344 to work on the truck for the last time. I felt sombre. I'd had a great run as a firefighter and had ended my career as a captain. I had taken a pummelling from the job, both physically and mentally, but it hadn't beaten me.

As I checked my mask and other equipment, I realized how different my life was going to be now that I wouldn't be with my firefighter family anymore. I rarely socialized outside of the job, unless it was with my buddies from the various fire stations I had worked at over the years. I hadn't anticipated the anxiety I was beginning to feel about leaving the job I had lived and loved for most of my life.

My crew — Derek Markey, Jacqui Kerrington, Shawn Tarasewicz, Jordan Muszynski, and Robin Earl — had organized a going-away party for me at the fire hall. Jacqui had called stations around the downtown core to let them know it was the last day for the Rat — a nickname I had for as long as I can remember. Cake and snacks for the informal drop-in were set up in the floor-watch room. I feel so honoured to have been able to work with such an amazing crew.

After I'd completed my equipment check, the department phone rang. It was my district chief, telling me that our truck had to go to the mechanical division for its semi-annual Department of Transportation inspection. On my last day? What about my party? After thirty-two years of service, my last shift would end with me watching mechanics grease up the fire truck? Fuck that!

I phoned the head of the mechanical division and told him what was going down at 344: a going-away party, for me!

"Yeah, sorry. You're due," he said.

"But it's my last day on the job after thirty-two years! I want to spend it with my crew."

"You'll still be with your crew here at mechanical." At that point I was winding up to pitch the phone across the street.

"Listen, can't you just reschedule it for tomorrow? It's my last day, mate."

"Then I'll have to reschedule tomorrow's trucks too," he countered.

"Yeah …?" I said, holding back the words *Go fuck yourself, matey!* in case I needed them.

He hemmed and hawed, but finally gave in. "Okay," he said.

Over the next few hours, trucks from across the downtown core dropped by to pass along their congratulations. Thirteen fire trucks and three chiefs went "on the air" to drive down to Fire Station 344 to say goodbye and good luck.

The next morning I shook hands with the incoming day-shift crew and said goodbye. I hugged my guys before packing the MINI Cooper with my gear for the last time. I drove home slowly, watching the sun come up.

As I walked into the house, Sue, my beautiful wife, was there, concerned, proud, and full of love for her former fire captain. She held me as I cried.

A week or so after I retired, one of the guys from my crew called to say our truck had been omitted from the post-incident review of the biggie because I hadn't sent in my report. I had written it, but got dispatched to a call just as I finished it and forgot to send it in. Shit.

I went back to visit the fire hall to log into the system and resubmit my report. But the system wouldn't let me log in — I no longer worked for Toronto Fire Services. I couldn't file my report. I guess you could say I had subconsciously left the door open. That way I could technically still be part of the fire department.

54

Postscript

WHEN I FIRST SAT DOWN to write my story, I didn't really understand how I would feel after I'd made it to retirement. I mean,
this was me: the firefighter, now and forever more. Now that I'm
retired, how do I define myself?

One month into retirement, I missed the job terribly. I sat alone
at home in my basement, smelling my smoky helmet and remembering the raging fires I had worn it in: the close calls, the exciting
times. One day, I took bagels and cream cheese to my old fire hall
to say hello to my crew. They weren't there. They were at a call for
a severed natural gas line.

As I walked around the hall, the first thing I was struck by was
the smell of smoke coming off the bunker gear. Funny, I'd never
noticed it before, but God, do I miss it. I miss feeling important.
I miss doing good. I miss my brothers and sisters. I miss being a
firefighter. But my time was over. The hurt of missing my job is
a privilege many of my firefighter brethren never get to suffer.
They die instead — gone before they get to hang up their helmets
and enjoy retirement.

Some days are harder than others. I still check the fire department website to see if the boys are at "a good one."

Neighbours ask, "Were you at that one?" when a big fire hits the news.

"No, I'm retired." But I tell them that my crew went, as if that made me a bit more impressive in their eyes and still worthy of their respect.

Sue is happy to have me home every night. She's glad she doesn't have to worry anymore whether I'm going to be hurt overnight at a fire. She's thankful to no longer be greeted in the morning by a husband with hurt in his eyes, suffering from having to deal with another dead person.

Because I was a firefighter, people have called me a hero. I'm not a hero; I was just a goalie trying to stop people from sliding through the Pearly Gates. Many more will follow me long after I'm gone.

One thing I've learned from being a firefighter — from the ups and downs, the good times and bad — is that life is like a stroll in the park. You get to appreciate the wonders of nature. You get to enjoy the warmth of the sun shining on your face. Then you step in a pile of dog shit. The stories will continue.

When I was a recruit riding the rigs in Yorkville in downtown Toronto, we stood up on the back of the fire truck. There were cab seats for the crew that were exposed to the elements; most guys used them only in the winter, tucking in behind the engine to keep warm.

It was spring, so I felt really good — a young kid working on his dream job with the wind blowing in his face. I was feeling like I'd finally made it. We were returning from a call when the truck turned north onto Bay Street. Way up the block, a little boy on the sidewalk, holding his mother's hand, was waving to the fire truck. Waving, waving, waving.

We finally approached this little guy after watching him wave for the entire length of the block. I casually waved back, and his face lit up. He absolutely beamed and then looked up at his mommy, sort of bouncing as he did.

I was a macho twenty-one-year-old, but tears came to my eyes. *My God, this is the most touching feeling I've ever experienced.* It shook me to be able to give a little boy so much joy with such a small gesture. That was the moment I knew I never wanted to be anything else. Over thirty years later, I still got that feeling when I saw a little one wave at a passing fire truck.

Acknowledgements

I OWE A DEBT OF gratitude to the many firefighters that came before me and to those smoke eaters that took me under their wings. Who taught me how to read the smoke and know when to back out.

I'm thankful to my wonderful publisher, Marc Coté, for his guidance and confidence in my ability to bring forth my story.

I have been blessed with the love of my beautiful and supportive wife Sue, two healthy and happy sons, Justin and Michael, and a pair of amazing stepchildren, Kyle and Kari — kids who are now grown up and hang out together, and who stood up for us very thankful parents on our wedding day on a beach in Aruba.

About the Author

BRYAN IS STILL BATTLING FLAMES in his memory and loving every minute of it. He also writes and produces for film and television. His first production under the banner Firehouse Mouse Productions was the children's video *Firetrucks and Firefighters*. After many years in distribution across North America it has been re-released as *Lots 'n' Lots of Fire Trucks* by Marshall Publishing delivering enjoyment to children from Africa to Australia and all points in between. He also produced the historical documentary *Iron Men, Wooden Ladders*, a story of heroism during the Great Toronto Fire of 1904, broadcast on the 100th anniversary of the disaster.

He spends his time off watching movies from Hollywood's Golden Age and walking his scruffy dog Molly in the Beaches area of Toronto.

We acknowledge the sacred land on which Cormorant Books operates. It has been a site of human activity for 15,000 years. This land is the territory of the Huron-Wendat and Petun First Nations, the Seneca, and most recently, the Mississaugas of the Credit River. The territory was the subject of the Dish With One Spoon Wampum Belt Covenant, an agreement between the Iroquois Confederacy and Confederacy of the Ojibway and allied nations to peaceably share and steward the resources around the Great Lakes. Today, the meeting place of Toronto is still home to many Indigenous people from across Turtle Island. We are grateful to have the opportunity to work in the community, on this territory.